Study Guide

for

Cunningham and Reich's

Culture and Values
A Survey of the Humanities

Sixth Edition

Ira Holmes
Central Florida Community College

THOMSON
WADSWORTH

Australia • Brazil • Canada • Mexico • Singapore • Spain • United Kingdom • United States

Printed in the United States of America

1 2 3 4 5 6 7 09 08 07 06 05

Printer: Thomson West

ISBN 0-534-58232-X

Cover image: Giovanni Antonio Canaletto (1697–1768). *The Rialto Bridge, Venice.* Louvre, Paris, France. Erich Lessing/Art Resource, NY.

Thomson Higher Education
10 Davis Drive
Belmont, CA 94002-3098
USA

TABLE OF CONTENTS

Preface vii

Tips for Effective Reading and Studying ix

Some Questions about the Humanities xi

Introduction to the Textbook xiii

Chapter 1: **The Beginnings of Civilization** 1
WEB QUESTS: Venus of Willendorf, Lascaux, Rosetta Stone, Egyptian Art, Gilgamesh, Storytelling, Hammurabi's Law Code 6

Chapter 2: **Early Greece** 9
WEB QUESTS: The Labyrinth, Daedalus and Icarus, Homer's *Odyssey*, Ancient Olympic Games 15

Chapter 3: **Classical Greece and the Hellenistic Period** 17
WEB QUESTS: Parthenon Marbles, History of the Marbles, Illustrated Greek Theater, Thespis 23

Chapter 4: **The Roman Legacy** 25
WEB QUESTS: Roman Empire in the First Century, Ovid's *Orpheus and Eurydice*, *Pygmalion*, The Pygmalion Phenomenon, The Pantheon, Trajan's Column 30

Chapter 5: **Ancient Civilizations of India and China** 33
WEB QUESTS: What Do Hindus Believe?, The Diamond Sutra, Tao Te Ching, "Buddha Mind" 39

End of Section Review of Ancient Civilizations 41

Chapter 6: **Jerusalem and Early Christianity** 43
WEB QUESTS: Dead Sea Scrolls, Ancient Manuscripts of the New Testament, Christians in the Age of Persecutions, Core Religious Beliefs: Judaism and Christianity, Pasolini's *Gospel of St. Matthew* 47

Chapter 7: **Byzantium** 49
WEB QUESTS: Hagia Sophia, Byzantine Icons, Saint Catherine's Monastery at Mount Sinai, *Codex Sinaiticus*, Symbols in Christian Art and Architecture 54

Chapter 8: **Islam** 57
WEB QUESTS: Islam: Empire of Faith, Islamic Art, Omar Khayyam's *Rubaiyat*, Sufism, Islam: The Qur'an – The Path Illuminated 62

Chapter 9: **Charlemagne and the Rise of Medieval Culture** 65
WEB QUESTS: The Complete Bayeux Tapestry 71

Chapter 10: **High Middle Ages: The Search for Synthesis** 73
WEB QUESTS: *The Canterbury Tales*, Becket, *The Divine Comedy* 79

Chapter 11: **The Fourteenth Century: A Time of Transition** 81
WEB QUESTS: *Les Très Riches Heures*, The Lion and the Unicorn Tapestries 86

End of Section Review of The Middle Ages 88

Chapter 12: **The Early Renaissance** 91
WEB QUESTS: Fra Angelico and Filippo Lippi's *Adoration of the Magi,* Leonardo da Vinci, *The Mona Lisa*, Why is the Mona Lisa Smiling? 97

Chapter 13: **The High Renaissance in Italy** 99
WEB QUESTS: Michelangelo, The Sistine Chapel "History Panels," Bellini's *Feast of the Gods* 104

Chapter 14: **The Renaissance in the North** 107
WEB QUESTS: Van Eyck's *Portrait of a Man,* Holbein's *The Ambassadors,* Bosch, Bruegel's *Children's Games* and *Netherlandisch Proverbs* 113

Chapter 15: **The Baroque World** 115
WEB QUESTS: Georges de la Tour, Rembrandt's Self Portraits, Vermeer, Versailles 122

Chapter 16: **The Eighteenth Century: From Rococo to Revolution** 125
WEB QUESTS: Fragonard, Hogarth's *Marriage à la Mode* 131

End of Section Review of Early Modern Europe 133

Chapter 17: **The Romantic Era** 137
WEB QUESTS: Casper David Friedrich, Goya's "Black Paintings" from the Quinta del Sordo, William Blake, Thoreau's *Walden*, Rosa Bonheur 144

Chapter 18: **Toward the Modern Era: 1870 – 1914** 147
WEB QUESTS: Van Gogh's Van Goghs, Rodin's *Hand of God*, Art Nouveau, Tanner's *Banjo Player*, Gauguin's *Where Do We Come From? What Are we? Where Are We Going?*, Klimt's *The Kiss*, Brancusi 154

Chapter 19: India, China, and Japan: From the Medieval to the Modern World 157
WEB QUESTS: Taj Mahal, Chinese Painting, Zen Stories 163

Chapter 20: The Peoples and Cultures of Africa 165
WEB QUESTS: Great Mosque of Djenne, Sankore Mosque at Timbuktu, Oral Tradition of the Griots, African Art, British Museum African Galleries 170

Chapter 21: Between the World Wars 173
WEB QUESTS: Duchamp's *Fountain,* René Magritte, George Grosz, Frida Kahlo, Salvador Dalí, Jacob Lawrence 180

Chapter 22: The Contemporary Contour 183
WEB QUESTS: Understanding Abstract Art, Georgia O'Keeffe, Andy Warhol, Judy Chicago, Maya Lin, David Hockney, Mark Tansey, Bill Viola, Faith Ringgold, Learning to Think Like an Artist 190

End of Section Review of Nineteenth and Twentieth Centuries 195

Final Review 201

Appendix A. Library Orientation 211

Appendix B. Finding Library Information 212

Appendix C. Humanities Internet Research 213

Appendix D. Evaluating Museum Web Sites 214

Appendix E. Writing Your Humanities Paper 215

Appendix F. Film Essay 217

Appendix G. Museum Visit 219

Appendix H. Audio Drama on the Internet 220

Appendix I. Recommended Books 221

Appendix J. Study Cards 223

PREFACE

Welcome. We're about to begin a journey in which we'll visit many of the greatest people and achievements of Western and non-Western civilizations. Just as real travelers to distant or unfamiliar lands often find it useful to have the services of a guide, who on the basis of experience or knowledge can offer assistance, so is this study guide designed to help you on your journey through the introductory humanities course.

As we travel, we need to be more than only tourists, wandering and sightseeing. We need also to wonder and to question. The subject of our wonder is humankind. What we are seeking is a better understanding of who we are as human beings, and why we act and think the way we do. In the humanities that understanding often comes from works of great thinkers, artists, and writers.

The sixteenth-century French essayist Montaigne once wrote that what matters in life is "not the destination, but the journey." He understood that it was not just getting to the last day that counted, but what happened along the way as we travel through our life. That's a good philosophy to apply to this course, its textbook, and this study guide.

The study guide is designed to help you reach your goal of being successful in this course. The study questions point out what's important. The thought questions encourage you to reflect on the meaning of what you've read. The self quizzes and exercises will help you retain knowledge by reviewing what you've learned. The information in the appendices offer additional opportunities for learning through the the Internet, great films on DVDs and videotapes, and, of course, books. There's also information on preparing and writing a humanities paper. Finally, the study cards at the end of the study guide are included to further test your knowledge of the text.

We have quite a trip ahead of us. But with planning and commitment we'll not only reach our goal but also have a meaningful journey along the way. As we travel, I ask you to have respect for those who are searching for truth, but to be wary of those who found it.

Bon Voyage!

Ira Holmes
Central Florida Community College

TIPS FOR EFFECTIVE READING AND STUDYING

LEARNING REQUIRES ACTIVITY, ESPECIALLY MENTAL ACTIVITY

- Quality reading means thinking/questioning as you physically move your eyes and turn the pages; true reading is a dialogue with the author.

- Afterwards, test yourself by closing the book and seeing how much you can recall.

  - "Close the book, and open your mind."

  - "You may learn more efficiently if the book is closed more often than it is open!"

  - Quality reading is more than mechanical reading.

SQ4R: EFFECTIVE STUDYING

S = SURVEY – Title, Introduction, Main Headings, Summary

Q = QUESTION – Form questions before reading
- Transform headings into questions
- Ask questions about the pictures

4R = READ – Actively
- Note important terms & ideas
- Try to answer your questions

RESTATE – Close the book and try to recall what you have just read; use a blank page and list what you can recall

REFLECT – Make sense of what you've read by relating it to your experiences or to what you already know

REVIEW – Go back over the material before you forget it—once is not enough! Review your notes, review without notes, and review regularly with a small study group of fellow students.

SELF QUIZ

1. Now that you've read the preceding page, <u>without going back to look at it</u>, make a brief list below of what you remember reading:

2. Go back and re-read the preceding page.

3. Now, how much can you recall:

4. **SQ<u>5</u>R: REWARD** yourself for good work (studying smart as well as studying hard).

SOME QUESTIONS ABOUT THE HUMANITIES

01. What are "the humanities"?

02. What college subjects (or disciplines) are included in the humanities?

03. What possible value do the humanities have in a practical age of technology and specialization?

04. Should the "humanities" be a required part of the college curriculum? Why? Why not?

05. Should there be a single required humanities course for all students, or should students be able to select a course from a list of "distribution requirements"?

06. What do you hope to gain from taking this humanities course?

07. How can stories, fact or fiction, help provide meaning for our lives?

08. What does a "good reader" contribute to the reading of a story or book, or the viewing of a painting (can pictures be read)?

09. Define "quality." What are some of the characteristics of "quality," for example, in buying a quality car or a quality house?

10. What are the signs of a quality student that could be observed by an instructor on the first day of class?

11. Is it true you get out of a job what you put into it? Out of a book? a painting? a college course? a relationship?

12. Briefly define:

    – Art

    – Aesthetics

    – History

    – Myth

I would describe the humanities as the best that has been said, thought, written, and otherwise expressed about the human experience.

– William J. Bennett

INTRODUCTION TO THE TEXTBOOK

The Arts: An Introduction

01. Which four arts are discussed in the Introduction?

02. What word does the text use to describe "works of human culture that have endured over the centuries"?

03. What word does the text use for works that not only have meaning for their own age but for subsequent generations?

04. In your own words, explain what the text means when it states that studying Greek tragedy (or really looking at art or closely reading literature) results in a "dialogue with our ancestors across the ages"?

05. Does it take careful listening to understand what people are really saying to us? To what books say? To what paintings say? (What is the difference between listening" and "hearing"? Between "looking" and "seeing"?

06. Are "movies" an "art"? Photography? Why or why not?

Discovering the Text

Chapter Illustrations

07. Look at the full-page illustrations beginning each chapter.

    a. Which one do you find the most interesting? Why?

    b. Which one do you find most beautiful? Why?

08. What are the titles of the full-page illustrations you selected (you will have to scan through the chapter to discover a smaller illustration that will include the title and information about the picture):

    Chapter ___:

    Chapter ___:

09. Thought Question: What do you think are the two or three criteria that determine the selection of works included in the textbook?

Pronunciation Guides

10. On which page in Chapter 1 can you find the right pronunciation for Akhenaton?

Glossary

11. On which pages in the textbook can be found the Glossary?

12. Define the below terms (try using your own words):

    Canon:

    Icon:

    Parable:

Index

13. Place a mark next to those artists included in the Index:

    _____ Angelou, Maya

    _____ Brancusi, Constantine

    _____ Bruegel, Pieter

    _____ Chicago, Judy

    _____ Delvaux, Paul

    _____ Friedrich, Casper David

    _____ Lawrence, Jacob

    _____ Kahlo, Frida

    _____ Klimt, Gustav

    _____ Monet, Claude

The humanities are ways of thinking about what is human.... When we ask who we are and what our lives ought to mean, we are using the humanities.

– American Association of Community and Junior Colleges
Humanities Policy Statement

1. THE BEGINNINGS OF CIVILIZATION

Study Questions:

THE EARLIEST PEOPLE AND THEIR ART

01. What are the six characteristics of civilized societies and of "civilization" mentioned in the textbook?

02. Which of these can be found also in lesser-developed human societies?

03. What practices of the Neanderthal people are considered an indication of the existence of religious beliefs?

04. Where can be found the oldest paintings (c. 15,000 – 13,000 B.C.E.) of humankind?

05. What visual art is even older (c. 28,000 – 23,000 B.C.E.) than the cave paintings at Lascaux and Altamira?

06. What was the subject matter of the oldest statues and statuettes?

07. What development during the Neolithic period made possible the growth of communities and villages?

ANCIENT MESOPOTAMIA

08. Why is it more difficult to generalize about ancient Mesopotamian culture than about ancient Egyptian? (Which word is more applicable to Ancient Mesopotamia, unity or diversity?)

09. In which civilization did the earliest form of writing develop? What was the name of this writing?

10. What was the first great literary work of ancient Mesopotamia?

11. What was the goal of the journey of Gilgamesh?

12. What was the subject of the story told by Utnapishtim in the *Epic of Gilgamesh*?

13. What three universal questions are touched upon in the *Epic of Gilgamesh?*

14. What type of building was the most important structure of the towns and cities of ancient Mesopotamia?

15. What was the subject of the cuneiform inscribed on the "Stele of Hammurabi"?

16. What were the subjects of the wall reliefs of the Assyrian palaces at Nimrud and Nineveh?

17. What civilization (ruled by Cyrus the Great) conquered the Assyrian Empire? How far east did the Persian Empire extend? How far west? Around 330 B.C.E., who conquered the Persians?

ANCIENT EGYPTIAN CIVILIZATION

18. What was the influence of the Egyptian god Aton-Ra on the chaos of the primeval universe?

19. Who was the first great architect known to history? What did he build?

20. What was the purpose of the pyramids of the Old Kingdom? What colossal statue stood next to the pyramids at Giza?

21. What was the most important religious idea of the New Kingdom of ancient Egypt? Which pharaoh is most associated with this concept?

22. What new capital city was established by Akhenaton?

23. What is the significance in the change of the name Amenhotep IV (<u>Amen</u>hotep) to Akhenaton (Akhen<u>aton</u>)?

24. How did the "Amarna art" of the pharaoh Akhenaton differ from conventional Egyptian art?

25. Which Queen of this period is the subject of perhaps the most famous of all Egyptian portraits? Who was her husband?

26. In the illustration of *Akhenaton, Nefertiti, and Three of Their Children* (Figure 1.15),

    a. Is the pharaoh shown as all powerful?

    b. What is the object depicted at the top center of the relief?

27. What event in 1923 increased the fame of Tutankhamen?

28. What adjective best describes the temples built by Ramses II at Luxor, Karnak, and Abu Simbel?

29. What was the most striking feature of the 3,000-year-old culture of ancient Egypt (especially in contrast with the history of the cultures of Mesopotamia)?

AEGEAN CULTURE

30. During the Bronze Age, what was the most important urban center of Aegean culture on Crete? On the mainland of Greece?

31. What was the most common subject of the art of the Cyclades islands?

32. Where and what was the Labyrinth? What was the Greek myth of the Minotaur, Theseus, and Ariadne?

33. Why did Sir Arthur Evans refer to Crete as Minoan civilization?

34. What two reasons did Evans give for his success as an archaeologist? (What is the lesson for us?)

35. Who was the central figure of Minoan religion?

36. What war provided the background for Homer's *Iliad* and *Odyssey*?

37. What were the two most important archaeological discoveries of Heinrich Schliemann? According to Schliemann, what city of Homer was buried beneath the Roman city of Ilium?

Thought Questions:

A. In Hammurabi's Law Code stated the principle of an "eye for an eye, a limb for a limb" should represent justice today? Do you think is still a good principle? Is there an alternative principle (for example, in Chapter 6)?

B. Egypt has been described as the "gift of the Nile"? Do you think the Nile was a "gift" or a "challenge" or both? Is a college education and this humanities course a gift or a challenge? Is life a gift or a challenge, or both?

C. The Egyptian god Aton-Ra imposed order on the chaos of the primeval universe. How do we in the twenty-first century impose some sense of order upon the chaos in our own lives?

D. The ancient Egyptians had conventions or expectations for what they considered "good art." What conventions or expectations do you have when you look for "good art"? Does society today still agree on conventions or expectations for "good art"?

E. What is a possible difference between a labyrinth and a maze? Which do you think is more likely to contain a path to follow for personal or spiritual transformation? For you, will this course be more of a labyrinth or a perplexing maze?

Define or Identify:

"Prehistoric"
- Paleolithic
- Neolithic (development of agriculture and settled communities)

ANCIENT MESOPOTAMIA
- "The land between the rivers": The Tigris and the Euphrates
- Sumer: The First Civilization
  - Uruk (Warka)
- Cuneiform

ANCIENT EGYPT: Old / Middle / New Kingdoms
- Nile River ("the gift of the Nile")
- Osiris / Isis / Horus
- Akhenaton
  - Monotheism
  - Amarna Art
- Hieroglyphics

AEGEAN CULTURES: Minoan / [Troy] / Mycenae
- Labyrinth

Significant Works To Recognize and Remember

Venus of Willendorf, c. 30,000 – 25000 B.C.E.
Lascaux Cave Paintings, c. 15,000 – 10,000 B.C.E.
Epic of Gilgamesh
Stele of Hammurabi's Law Code
Ziggurat at Ur
Lady of Warka
Assyrian Wall Reliefs
Imhotep, Step Pyramid of Zoser
Sphinx & Pyramids at Giza
Bust of Queen Nefertiti
Cycladic Statues
Palace of Minos, Knossos
Minoan Snake Goddesses

Other Important Works (Not in the textbook)

Chauvet Caves, c. 31,000 B.C.E.
Palette of Narmer, c. 2700 B.C.E.
Stonehenge, c. 2000 B.C.E.
Rosetta Stone, 196 B.C.E.

CHAPTER 1 - REVIEW

Begin by writing the title of the chapter you've just studied. Next, without looking at the text or your study guide, use your memory to recall and to list the major sections or topics covered in the chapter. Finally, check your knowledge by taking the short "Self Quiz" below.

A) CHAPTER TITLE:

B) MAJOR SECTIONS OR TOPICS:

C) SELF QUIZ # 1 – IDENTIFY THE:

01. ________________ Subject of the statue from Willendorf, c. 30,000 B.C.E.

02. ________________ Caves containing humankind's earliest paintings.

03. ________________ First architect known to history; he built the earliest pyramid in Egypt.

04. ________________ New Kingdom Pharaoh advocating monotheism; his Queen was Nefertiti.

05. ________________ Hero of the most famous Sumerian epic; he traveled on a journey in quest of the meaning of life.

06. ________________ System of writing ("wedge-shaped") used by the ancient Sumerians.

07. ________________ Author of the great law code of ancient Babylon ("an eye for an eye").

08. ________________ Civilization famous for the wall reliefs of hunting scenes on its palaces at Nimrud and Nineveh.

09. ________________ Most important subject of Cycladic art.

10. ________________ A place full of intricate passageways; in Greek mythology the place where the Minotaur was confined, and later killed by Theseus with the help of Ariadne.

1. WEB QUESTS - PREHISTORY, MESOPOTAMIA, EGYPT

WOMEN IN PREHISTORY: VENUS OF WILLENDORF
http://witcombe.sbc.edu/willendorf/willendorfdiscovery.html

01. In what year was the Venus of Willendorf discovered? In what city is it now displayed?

02. How old is the Venus of Willendorf (according to the 1990 estimate)?

03. *[Click on "What's in a Name" to advance to the next web page.]* What was the name of the classical goddess of sexual love and beauty? What was the Greek name of this goddess?

04. What is the meaning of the statement that "the 'Venus' of Willendorf is visibly biologically female, but she is not feminine"?

05. *[Click on "Woman from Willendorf" to advance to the next web page.]* What is the advantage of calling her the "Woman from Willendorf" rather than the "Venus of Willendorf"?

LASCAUX
http://www.culture.fr/culture/arcnat/lascaux/fr/

06. *[Use the cursor/flashlight to explore the images on the wall of the cave.]* What images can you see on the wall of the cave?

07. [*Click on one of the images, then click on "English" [in the lower left-hand corner] to read the English language version.]* What images of animals have been found in Lascaux?

08. Why was Lascaux closed in 1963? Why was Lascaux II opened in 1983?

THE ROSETTA STONE
http://www.ancientegypt.co.uk/writing/home.html

09. What is the importance of the Rosetta Stone?

10. When and where was it discovered?

11. What three distinct scripts are found on the stone?

12. Who was the French scholar primarily responsible for the translation of the Rosetta Stone?

ANCIENT EGYPTIAN ART: INTRODUCTION – FUNERARY SCENE
http://www.shira.net/ancient-scenes.htm

13. Who are the fourteen people (facing left) at the top?

14. Why is the deceased person being led to the scale by the jackal god Anubis?

15. How will the feather of Ma'at decide the future of the deceased?

16. Who is the god of wisdom standing to the right of the scale?
Why is he holding a scroll in his hands?

17. Who is the lord of the underworld (sitting on the throne to the right)?

18. What symbol of immortality (the key to life eternal) is held by both Anubis and Horus?

GILGAMESH
http://www.wsu.edu/~dee/MESO/GILG.HTM
Read the Introduction (first paragraph), and then scroll down to read Richard Hooker's summary of Tablets 1 and 11.

19. Who was king of Uruq (Iraq) around 2700 B.C.E.?

20. How many stone tablets were used to record the fullest version we have of Gilgamesh? In what Assyrian city were they discovered?

21. What is the subject of Tablet 11?

"STORYTELLING, THE MEANING OF LIFE" AND THE EPIC OF GILGAMESH", AN ESSAY BY ARTHUR A. BROWN
http://eawc.evansville.edu/essays/brown.htm

22. According to Brown's first paragraph, what are two reasons to read or hear the story of Gilgamesh?

23. According to Brown's paragraph 14 (beginning with the words: "Beside the sea, Gilgamesh meets Siduri, 'the woman of the river, the maker of wine.' "), what should Gilgamesh do with the gift of his life?

HAMMURABI'S LAW CODE
http://eawc.evansville.edu/anthology/hammurabi.htm

For each of the situations below,
(a) briefly describe what you think would be a just solution, then

(b) look up the appropriate law in by clicking on the below underlined specific laws and briefly summarizing them.

24. What would should be done in each of the following situations:
a) someone in a fight puts out the eye of another ?
– Your Response:

– Hammurabi's Response (Law #196)

b) a boy slaps hard his father?
– Your Response:

– Hammurabi's Response (Law #195)

c) a son is adopted and then the natural parents want him back?
– Your Response:

– Hammurabi's Response (Law #185)

25. Which, if any, of the above laws do you think should be in effect today?

OPTIONAL: CAUTION!! BEWARE OF THE MINOTAUR!
http://www.logicmazes.com/theseus.html

Can you escape from the labyrinth and its dreadful minotaur? Try your skill (or luck) by clicking on the above link. You will be Theseus (the red dot), and you must escape from a series of mazes. There is also a mechanical Minotaur (the black dot) in each maze. For every turn that Theseus takes, the Minotaur takes two turns. Use the arrows on your keyboard to navigate. ***GOOD LUCK!***

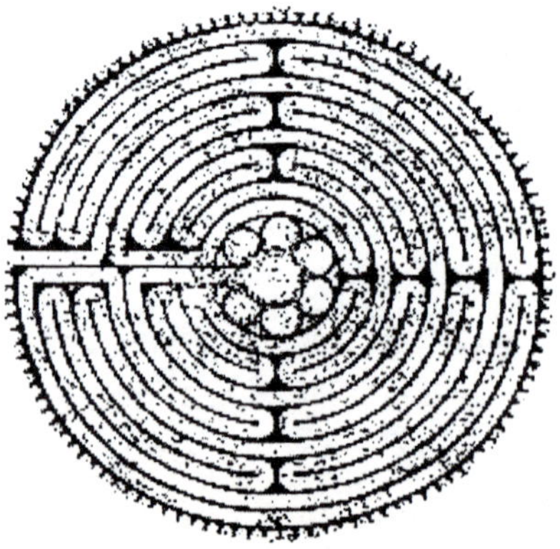

2. *EARLY GREECE*

Study Questions:

INTRODUCTION

01. What two epic poems became the first great works of literature of "early Greece"?

02. What war marks the end of the period of "early Greece" and the beginning of the "Classical period"?

HOMER AND THE HEROIC AGE

03. What was the *polis*? In what sense was the *polis* both the glory and the ruin of Greek civilization?

04. What book in Greek religion was the equivalent of the Old and New Testaments?

05. Which Greek deity represented the

– father of the gods (ruling from Mt. Olympus):

– daughter of Zeus and goddess of intelligence:

– goddess of beauty and love:

06. What two opposing aspects of Greek civilization were represented by Apollo and Dionysus? Are the two forces represented by Apollo and Dionysus also part of our "human nature"?

07. Which Greek god represented supreme good? Supreme evil?

08. For the ancient Greeks, what was the role of art and literature in examining the problems of human morality?

09. Who was the first known "author" in the history of western literature? What were his achievements?

10. Which Greek epic tells the story of the siege of Troy (Ilium)?

11. According to the *Iliad*, what was the lesson of the anger of Achilles (and other mortals)?

12. According to Zeus in Book One of *The Odyssey*, why is it unjust for men to blame the gods for human suffering ("How foolish men are!")?

13. What is the meaning of the word *odyssey*?

ART, ARCHITECTURE, AND MUSIC

14. Why is painted pottery emphasized in the study of the first three hundred years of Greek art?

15. What was the *meander* found on Greek geometric pottery?

16. By the eighth century B.C.E., what had become the principal subject of Greek art?

17. What was the purpose of the *amphora* (figure 2.2) with a hole in its base?

18. What figures are found on the main decorative band of the *Dipylon Amphora* (figure 2.3) to reinforce the belief this was used as a grave marker?

19. How did the technique of red-figured style vases compare with the earlier black-figured technique?

20. What facial expression is found on the *Peplos Kore* (figure 2.10)?

21. How did the clothing of the *kouros* differ from that of the *kore*?

22. What is the difference between high relief and low relief sculpture?

23. In architecture, what style or order is associated with the Archaic period of Greece? the Classical period? with Roman architecture?

24. In Doric architecture, what were the triglyphs? the metopes?

25. How did the Doric differ from the Ionic style or order of architecture?

	Doric	Ionic
– the base?		
– the capital?		
– the frieze?		

26. In Greek music, what was the doctrine of *ethos*?

EARLY GREEK LITERATURE, PHILOSOPHY AND HISTORY

27. Who was the first woman to leave a literary record of her personal feelings and opinions (in lyric poetry)?

28. What is the literal meaning of the word "philosophy"?

29. What is the subject of the following branches of philosophy:

    – Logic

    – Political Philosophy

    – Aesthetics

    – Ethics

    – Epistemology

    – Metaphysics

30. Which pre-Socratic philosopher

    – tried to explain all phenomenon in terms of one or more material elements?

    – believed that mathematical relationships represented the underlying principle of the universe?

    – believed that our world was subject to constant change ("It is not possible to step into the same river twice.")?

    – taught that "Man is the measure of all things"?
    [What other measure could there be?]

31. Why did the Persian king Darius invade Greece?

32. What were the famous "wooden walls" of Athens?

33. Who was the first great Greek historian (the "Father of History")? What was the title of his famous "historia"?

34. According to Herodotus, why were the Persians defeated? What Greek word does he use for his explanation? What is the English translation of this word?

35. What new age in Greek history began with the Greek victory in the Persian Wars?

36. Review: Who was the most famous Greek author of

– epics?

– lyric poetry?

– history?

Thought Questions:

A. The ancient Greeks saw literature and drama as a source for understanding the human condition. Do you think the contemporary arts provide a similar role? Which of today's arts (literature, theater, music, etc.) do you find the most meaningful?

B. In what sense are all humans on an odyssey?

C. Should contemporary historians make moral judgments (like Herodotus) or should they be more impartial, objective, and scientific?

Abundance of knowledge does not teach us to be wise. – Heracleitus

Define or Identify:

Polis
Homer
- *Iliad*
- *Odyssey*

Apollo vs. Dionysus
Human reason / Divine revelation

Geometric Art
- Meander pattern

Black-figured Vases / Red-figured Vases
Kore
Kouros

Relief (High, Low)
Architecture
- Styles
  - Doric
  - Ionic
  - Corinthian
- Frieze
  - Metopes
  - Triglyph

Pediment

Sappho

Pre-Socratic philosophers
- Thales of Miletus
- Pythagoras
- Heracleitus
- Protagoras

Historians
- Herodotus, *History of the Persian Wars*

Hubris

Significant Works to Recognize and Remember

Kouros, c. 530 B.C.E.
Peplos Kore, c. 530 B.C.E.

CHAPTER 2 - REVIEW

Begin by writing the title of the chapter you've just studied. Next, without looking at the text or your study guide, use your memory to recall and to list the major sections or topics covered in the chapter. Finally, check your knowledge by taking the short "Self Quiz" below.

A) CHAPTER TITLE:

B) MAJOR SECTIONS OR TOPICS:

C) SELF QUIZ # 2 – IDENTIFY THE:

01. ______________ Author of the *Iliad* and the *Odyssey.*

02. ______________ Greek word for city; used for the independent city-states of ancient Greece.

03. ______________ Greek god representing logic, order, and the power of the rational mind.

04. ______________ Greek god of the emotions and of wine.

05. ______________ Male standing statue, usually nude, made in early Greece.

06. ______________ Earliest style or order of Greek temple architecture, simple and austere; the columns had no base and the frieze was divided into triglyphs and metopes.

07. ______________ Greek lyric poet and the first woman to leave a literary record that reflected her own personal experiences (*Poems*).

08. ______________ First Greek Historian (the "Father of History"); author of the *History of the Persian Wars.*

09. ______________ Greek word for excessive pride or ambition.

10. ______________ Pre-Socratic philosopher best known for his teaching, "Man is the measure …."

2. WEB QUESTS - EARLY GREECE

THE LABYRINTH, THE MINOTAUR, THESEUS AND ARIADNE
http://www.minotaur-websites.com/minomyth.htm#theseus

01. On what island does the story begin? Who was the king of this island? Where was his palace located?

02. Who built a hollow wooden cow to help Queen Pasiphaë? What was the product of the union of Queen Pasiphaë with the white bull sent to Crete by Poseidon, god of the sea?

03. What was the physical appearance of the Minotaur?

04. For what purpose did King Minos build the Labyrinth? Who designed the Labyrinth?

05. Why did Theseus of Athens go to Crete?

06. Who was the daughter of King Minos? How did she help Theseus find his way out of the Labyrinth?

07. What was the fate of Ariadne?

08. Why did King Aegeus of Athens throw himself into the sea (now called the Aegean) when he saw the returning ship of his son?

DAEDALUS AND ICARUS
http://www.dl.ket.org/humanities/literature/litpacket/metamorphoses.htm
[*Read the fate of Daedalus and Icarus in this new and moving translation from Ovid's* Metamorphoses *by Rolphe Humphries.]*

09. How did Daedalus plan to escape from Crete? Who was his son? What advice did he give his son? (Lines 23–26)

10. How does the advice of Daedalus compare with the motto of the ancient Greeks "Nothing in Excess"?

11. What was the fate of Icarus? Why?

12. In your opinion, what was the most moving and emotional line?

VISIT: HOMER – THE ODYSSEY
http://mfile.akamai.com/34/wmv/covery.download.akamai.com/34/dcol/school/2001/08/08/ancientgreece.asx

http://mfile.akamai.com/34/rm/covery.download.akamai.com/34/dcol/school/2001/08/08/ancientgreece.ram

The first site uses Windows Media Player; the second is for Real One Player. Media Player probably came with and is installed on your computer. This WebQuest provides a choice, but many sites still offer only the Real One Player. The Real Player is available free, but you have to be careful. Click on this link: www.real.com. CLICK on the word "FREE." On the next page, CLICK on "Download Free Real Player." Be aware that the "Premium Player with Super Pass" is not free.

Be prepared for many free advertisements. OR, try this new site available from NPR's Car Talk: http://www.real.com/freeplayer/?rppr=cartalk.com

13. What word, which comes to us from the Greek, meant "stories that people told to explain the world around them"?

14. How many years was the journey ("odyssey") of Odysseus to Ithaca and to his wife Penelope? How long should the journey have taken?

15. What did Odysseus want to be able to say when he reached his deathbed and the end of his life? ("Man, I _____ __ _____.")

THE REAL STORY OF THE ANCIENT OLYMPIC GAMES
http://www.upenn.edu/museum/Olympics/olympicintro.html

16. "Early Athletes: Amateurs or Pros?" What was the meaning of the ancient Greek word athlete?

17. What would the ancient Greeks think of the concept of "amateur athletics"?

18. "Were the Ancient Olympics Just for Men?" Were women allowed to compete?

19. "Glossary" Identify the correct term for:

    A. __________________ One who competes for a prize

    B. __________________ Place of naked people

    C. __________________ Victory; goddess of victory.

3. *CLASSICAL GREECE AND THE HELLENISTIC PERIOD*

Study Questions:

INTRODUCTION – THE CLASSICAL IDEAL

01. What name is given to the period of Greek history between the Persian Wars and Alexander the Great?

02. What descriptive name has been given to the Athenian civilization of the last half of the fifth century B.C.E.?

03. Why are Greek tragedies still read and performed?

04. What influence did the Macedonians and Romans have on the spread of Greek ideas?

05. What name is given to the period of history following the death of Alexander the Great in 323 B.C.E. (and until the rise of the Roman Empire)?

07. What was the "dark side" of the Greek "spirit"?

08. What was the role of reason in imposing a sense of order on the chaos of the world?

09. Why was the Greek belief in "nothing in excess" important in avoiding hubris?

10. Why did the Greeks emphasize the study of human thought and actions?

11. What was the result of the victory in the Persian War on Athenian civilization?

12. What was the purpose of the Delian League according to Athens? According to the other Greek city-states?

13. What was the cause of the Peloponnesian War? the eventual result of the war?

14. What great historian wrote the *History of the Peloponnesian War*? Why was he a great historian?

15. According to Thucydides, which leader is most associated with the achievements of the Athenian Golden Age?

DRAMA IN CLASSICAL GREECE

16. Who were the three great masters of Classical Greek drama?

17. What literary form evolved from the choral hymns sung in honor of the Greek god Dionysus?

18. Who was the first important Athenian tragic dramatist (the *Oresteia* trilogy)? What does the *Oresteia* trilogy say about the way to bring a rational society of human beings out of primeval chaos?

19. Who was the author of *Antigone* and *Oedipus the King*?

20. Why did Antigone disobey King Creon?

21. What action did Oedipus take regarding his father? his mother? According to the Greeks, why did Oedipus deserve to suffer for his actions?

22. Which Greek dramatist showed the most sympathy for the problems of women (*Medea, Phaedra*) who lived in a society dominated by men?

23. Who was the greatest Greek author of comedy plays?

24. In Aristophanes' *Lysistrata*, what action did the women of Athens take to convince men to stop their war?

PHILOSOPHY IN THE LATE CLASSICAL PERIOD

25. How much of our knowledge of Socrates comes from his own writings? from the works of his student Plato?

26. What was the method used by Socrates to test the truth of traditional ideas?

27. How did Socrates' opponents feel about their ignorance being exposed by the questions of Socrates? (How do people today feel about their ignorance being exposed?)

28. What institution, founded by Plato in 387 B.C.E., was the first permanent institution in western civilization devoted to education and research?

29. What was Plato's "Theory of Forms"? What does his theory say about the world we perceive around us?

30. Who was Plato's most gifted student?

31. What school was founded by Aristotle in 335 B.C.E. (in competition with Plato's Academy)?

32. What was "real" according to Plato? to Aristotle?

33. How did Aristotle resolve Plato's split between the apparent reality we perceive and the genuine reality acquired by philosophical contemplation?

34. According to Aristotle, what caused the downfall of tragic heroes? What was the result on the audience of watching the fate of the tragic hero?

35. Why did Plato advocate the censorship of music? (Do you agree? Why?)

THE VISUAL ARTS

36. What was the subject of the *Canon* by Polykleitos? What did Polykleitos mean by a "canon of proportion"? (Would this understanding of the importance of proportion and scale to beauty also apply to architecture?)

37. Why is the Parthenon an "incomparable symbol of the Golden Age of Greece"?

38. How did the building of the Parthenon contribute to the Peloponnesian War?

39. For which goddess was the Parthenon built?

40. What was the subject of the Parthenon frieze (the Elgin Marbles)?

41. In what city and what museum are the Elgin Marbles located?

42. What is the subject of the caryatids of the Erectheum?

43. Why was the nude statue of *Aphrodite of Cyrene* by Praxiteles important in the history of western art?

THE HELLENISTIC PERIOD

44. What was the influence of Alexander the Great on the spread of Greek ideas to Syria, Egypt, and India?

45. What two events mark the beginning and the end of the Hellenistic Period?

46. What was the greatest city of the Hellenistic Age? What was the most important city of Hellenistic <u>Asia</u>?

47. How did Hellenistic art differ from Classical art? Which style emphasized order and balance? Which style emphasized emotion and expression?

48. What was the subject of the frieze on the *Altar to Zeus* at Pergamum?

49. What story was told by the *Laocoön* sculpture?

50. Into which empire were the Hellenistic cities absorbed?

Thought Questions:

A. In what sense can it be said that Rome was conquered by Greece?

B. Which do you think is more important, obeying the law of the land, or following your own individual conscience if you think the law is unjust? Would you be more like Creon or Antigone? Why?

C. Socrates describes himself as a "midwife to ideas"? Does a midwife create what she delivers? Do you think ideas created or preexistent?

D. Should the Elgin Marbles be returned to Greece so they can be viewed in their country of origin? Why? (What about other works of art that have been removed from Egypt, Mesopotamia, and other countries?)

E. Aristotle was considered the "greatest systemizer." Systematizing and classifying can help in understanding knowledge. How can you classify or organize the information in this course (or in life) in order to know and understand it better?

F. Praxiteles (*Aphrodite of Cyrene* and *Hermes with the Infant Dionysus*) showed the nude human body as an object of beauty. Should the nude body be seen as beautiful or shameful? (What is the difference between "nude" and "naked"?)

History is philosophy teaching by example. – Thucydides

Define or Identify:

The Golden Age of Greece
- Pericles

Persian Wars
Peloponnesian Wars
Thucydides, *History of the Peloponnesian Wars*

Aeschylus, *Oresteia* trilogy (Agamemnon)
Sophocles, *Oedipus, Antigone*
Euripides, *Medea*
"Tragedy"
hamartia
Aristophanes, *Lysistrata*
Polykleitos, *The Canon*

"Philosophy"
- Socrates
- Plato: Ideas / Forms (The Ideal as Reality)
  - *The Republic*
  - Academy
- Aristotle: Classification of Knowledge
  - Lyceum
  - *Catharsis*

Hellenistic Age
- Alexander the Great
- Alexandria
- Pergamum

Significant Works To Recognize and Remember

Acropolis
- Parthenon (Elgin Marbles), 447–432 B.C.E.
  - Frieze
  - Metopes
- Erechtheum (Porch of the Maidens - Caryatids), 421–406 B.C.E.

Myron, *Discus Thrower*, 450 BC
Polykleitos, *Spear-bearer (Doryphoros)*, c. 450–440 B.C.E.
Altar to Zeus, Pergamum ("Athena Slaying Giants"), c. 180 B.C.E.
Praxiteles, *Aphrodite of Cyrene* (Female Nude), c. 100 B.C.E.
Laocoön (and His Two Sons), early first century C.E.

Other Important Works (Not in the textbook)
Victory of Samothrace / Winged Victory, c. 190 B.C.E.
Venus de Milo, c. 100 B.C.E.

CHAPTER 3 - REVIEW

Begin by writing the title of the chapter you've just studied. Next, without looking at the text or your study guide, use your memory to recall and to list the major sections or topics covered in the chapter. Finally, check your knowledge by taking the short "Self Quiz" below.

A) CHAPTER TITLE:

B) MAJOR SECTIONS OR TOPICS:

C) SELF QUIZ # 3 – IDENTIFY THE:

01. ________________ Author of the *History of the Peloponnesian War*, his impartiality made him the first objective, scientific historian.

02. ________________ Leader during the Golden Age of Athens; he made visible the glory of Athens by constructing magnificent new buildings atop the Acropolis.

04. ________________ Author of *Oedipus the King* and *Antigone*.

04. ________________ Best known student of Socrates, author of *the Dialogues, The Apology, The Republic*, and founder of the Academy.

05. ________________ "Great systemizer," founder of the Lyceum, and the best-known student of Plato.

06. ________________ Most famous and beautiful building on top of the Acropolis in Athens.

07. ________________ Columns in the shape of young women on the Porch of the Maidens of the Erectheum.

08. ________________ Name of the period of Greek culture from the death of Alexander the Great to the Roman conquest of Greece.

09. ________________ Greatest city of the Hellenistic Age.

10. ________________ Wealthiest city of Hellenistic Asia; its chief shrine was an immense Altar to Zeus showing the battle between the gods and the giants.

3. WEB QUESTS - CLASSICAL GREECE

THE PARTHENON MARBLES
http://www.greece.org/parthenon/marbles/pmarb.htm

01. What three sets of sculpture decorate the Parthenon?

    A. _______________ Individual sculptures in high relief?

    B. _______________ One long continuous sculpture in low relief?

    C. _______________ Sculptures in the round (not relief) filling the triangular spaces at both ends of the Parthenon?

02. What was the name of the simple architectural decoration separating the metopes from each other?

03. What was the subject of the metopes on the

    A. south side of the Parthenon?

    B. east side of the Parthenon?

    C. west side of the Parthenon?

04. What was the subject of the frieze placed above the inner row of columns?

05. What forty-foot high statue was housed inside the Parthenon?

06. Of the surviving panels in the frieze, where are thirty-six found today?

07. Where are another fifty-six panels located?

08. Of the surviving metopes, where are thirty-nine located today?

09. Where are the other fifteen located?

10. What is the position of the Greek government about the Parthenon Marbles? Why?

THE HISTORY OF THE MARBLES
http://www.greece.org/parthenon/marbles/history0.htm

11. Why in 479 B.C.E. did Pericles and the Athenians want to construct new buildings such as the Parthenon on the Acropolis?

12. What was the fate of the Parthenon in 450 C.E.?

13. After the arrival of the Turks in 1458, what was the fate of the Parthenon?

14. In 1687, how was the Parthenon impacted by the Venetian army?

15. Between 1801 and 1816, what was the influence of Lord Elgin on the Parthenon? (*See Part 2*)

16. What recent developments have there been with the Elgin / Parthenon Marbles? (*Click on "Campaign Update"*)

DR. J's ILLUSTRATED GREEK THEATER
http://lilt.ilstu.edu/drjclassics/lectures/theater/ancient_greek_theater.shtm

17. What may have been the importance of the Theater of Dionysus in Athens?

18. What was the original purpose of the circular area called the "orchestra"?

19. Compare the Greek meaning of *theaomai* and *theatron* with the Roman "auditorium"?

20. What was the approximate seating capacity of an ancient Greek theater?

21. What was the *skene*?

22. Where were murders and other violent acts usually performed?

THESPIS
http://en.wikipedia.org/wiki/Thespis

23. Who was Thespis? Why is he important in the history of theater?

4. *THE ROMAN LEGACY*

Study Questions:

EARLY ROME (THE ROMAN REPUBLIC)

01. What was the Roman contribution to Western civilization, for example,

    a) the alphabet?
    b) the calendar?
    c) art and literature?
    d) Christian Church?

02. What did the Romans value more, good government and military prowess, or cultural and artistic achievements?

04. What are the two main periods of Roman history?

    – 509 to 31 B.C.E.:
    – 31 B.C.E. to C.E. 476:

05. What people occupied Rome from 616 to 510 B.C.E.? What is the name for the part of Italy ruled by these people?

07. What event marks the beginning of the history of the Roman Republic?

08. What Roman class was represented in the Senate?

09. What was the name of the large open space in the center of Rome used for meetings of the Senate and the assemblies of the people?

11. What events in the last hundred years of the Roman Republic would cause many Romans to welcome the rule of an emperor such as Augustus?

12. What were the two principal schools of philosophy in Rome? Where did they originate?

13. According to Epicurus, what is the goal of human actions?

14. According to Epicurus, why should humans be able to live free from superstitious fear of the unknown and not have to fear the threat of divine retribution?

16. Which Greco-Roman philosophy taught the value of self-control in acquiring virtue? (Why is it considered Greco-Roman and not just Roman?)

17. What Greco-Roman philosophy is associated with Seneca, Epictetus, and Marcus Aurelius?

18. What was the subject of the *Ius Civile* of Julius Caesar?

19. What were the Roman equivalent to the Greek gods:

– Zeus = – Aphrodite =

– Hera = – Athena =

– Poseidon = – Hermes =

– Apollo = – Dionysus =

20. What large public meeting place was built in Rome by Julius Caesar?

21. What military events characterized the last century of the Roman Republic (133 B.C.E. to 31 B.C.E.)? [See text summary]

THE ROMAN EMPIRE: 31 B.C.E. – C.E. 476

22. What was the significance of the Battle of Actium (31 B.C.E.) in the history of the Roman Republic?

23. Who was the first emperor of the Roman Empire?

24. Which emperor is best associated with the Golden Age of the Roman Empire?

25. What new title did Octavian assume in 27 B.C.E.?

26. Who was the greatest of all Roman poets? For what work is he best known? Who was Emperor at the time it was written?

27. What epic poem was to Roman literature what the *Iliad* and the *Odyssey* were to Greek literature?

28. In Vergil's *Aeneid* (written during the reign of Augustus), what seems to be the lesson of the tragic love affair between Dido and Aeneas?

29. According to the *Ara Pacis* (*Altar of Peace*), how did Augustus want to be seen by his contemporaries, and to be remembered by future generations?

30. What town, 150 miles south of Rome and destroyed by an eruption of Mt. Vesuvius in C.E. 79, has provided immense information about life in the early Roman Empire?

31. The capture of what city in Judea was commemorated by the Arch of Titus (C.E. 81)?

32. What invention in the first century B.C.E. made possible the Roman use of barrel vaults and domes?

33. What emperor designed the Pantheon (C.E. 126)? What was architecturally significant about the shape of its roof? What was the function of its oculus?

34. Which style did Roman architecture prefer to the Doric and Ionic? How did this style different from the Doric and Ionic?

35. What were some of the targets of Juvenal's *Satires*?

36. What event in C.E. 476 marks the formal end of the Roman Empire in Western Europe?

37. What was the significance of the founding of Constantinople in C.E. 330?

38. In what sense did the Roman Empire survive until C.E. 1453?

39. Who were the two most important rulers of the Late Roman Empire in the West, and what was their most important achievement?

    - C.E. 284 – 305:

    - C.E. 306 – 337:

Thought Questions:

A. What lesson may there be for us in the Roman genius in absorbing and assimilating external cultures?

B. Which do you think is more difficult to deal with, fear of the known or fear of the unknown?

C. Is there more than one lesson from the story of Dido and Aeneas? [How should people resolve the conflict between personal satisfaction and social responsibility?]

D. Augustus preferred to be viewed not as emperor but as the "first citizen" of Rome or as "first among equals" as a member of the Senate. What are the advantages of being both first and equal?

Define or Identify:

Etruscans / Tuscany
Roman Republic: 509 B.C.E. – 31 B.C.E.
Roman Empire: 31 B.C.E. – C.E. 476

Caesar
    Ius Civile

Greco-Roman Philosophies
    Epicureanism (Epicurus)
    Stoicism
Marcus Aurelius, *Meditations*

Octavian / Augustus ["First Among Equals"]
    Battle of Actium, 31 B.C.E.
    Vergil, *Aeneid*
Pompeii, C.E. 79
    Juvenal, *Satires*

Corinthian Architecture

Constantine
Constantinople ("New Rome") C.E. 330
C.E. 476: Last Roman Emperor in the West
C.E. 1453: Fall of Constantinople to the Turks

Significant Works To Recognize and Remember

Forum of Rome
Ara Pacis (Altar of Peace), 13–9 B.C.E.
Arch of Titus, C.E. 70
Pantheon, Rome (Oculus), C.E. 126
Colosseum, C.E. 80
Arch of Constantine, c. C.E. 312
Basilica of Constantine, Rome, C.E. 306–315

Other Important Works (Not in the textbook)

Trajan's Column, C.E. 113
Ovid, *Metamorphoses* (Theseus, Pygmalion. Narcissus)

Only the educated are free. – Epictetus

CHAPTER 4 - REVIEW

Begin by writing the title of the chapter you've just studied. Next, without looking at the text or your study guide, use your memory to recall and to list the major sections or topics covered in the chapter. Finally, check your knowledge by taking the short "Self Quiz" below.

A) CHAPTER TITLE:

B) MAJOR SECTIONS OR TOPICS:

C) SELF QUIZ # 4 – IDENTIFY THE:

01. a. ______________ First period of Roman history (from 509 to 31 B.C.E.).

b. ______________ Second half of Roman history (from 31 B.C.E. to C.E. 476).

02. ______________ Public meeting place of the Romans, including the Senate and the assemblies of the people.

03. ______________ Greco-Roman philosophy founded by Epicurus that taught the goal of life was the pursuit of pleasure, but with moderation and with prudence.

04. ______________ Greco-Roman philosophy founded by Xeno that taught the value of self control in acquiring virtue.

05. ______________ First great emperor of Rome; he saw himself as "first among equals."

06. ______________ Greatest Roman Poet, author of the *Aeneid.*

07. ______________ Roman building designed by Hadrian; it had a 142-foot high rotunda, topped by a concrete dome with an oculus.

08. ______________ Order of architecture (decorated with acanthus leaves) preferred by Romans, rather than Doric and Ionic.

09. ______________ New city, built by the Emperor Constantine in C.E. 330, which became the capital Empire in the East.

10. ______________ Year marking the last Roman Emperor in the West and the end of the Roman Empire in the West.

4. WEB QUESTS - ANCIENT ROME

THE ROMAN EMPIRE IN THE FIRST CENTURY
http://www.pbs.org/empires/romans/voices/index.html

01. What work by Virgil became a national epic honoring Rome and prophesying the rise of the Roman Empire?

02. Who was the great hero (he was the embodiment of Roman ideals—loyalty to the state, devotion to family, and reverence for the gods) of Virgil's *Aeneid*?

03. *Click on "Ovid" to advance to the next page.* What was the subject of Ovid's *Ars Amatoria*?

04. How did the Emperor Augustus reward Ovid for his *The Art of Love*?

05. Which work by Ovid became an epic poem that combined myth and history to tell the story of the Roman world from its beginning to the time of Tiberius?

OVID'S ORPHEUS AND EURYDICE
http://www.paleothea.com/Myths/Orpheus.html

06. In Ovid's telling of the story of Orpheus and Eurydice:

- Why did Orpheus descend to the underworld?
- Orpheus' request was granted, but with what condition?
- What action did Orpheus take upon reaching the threshold of the upper world?
- What then was the fate of Eurydice?

OVID'S PYGMALION
http://www.mythfolklore.net/3043mythfolklore/reading/ovid/pages/09.htm

07. In Ovid's *Pygmalion and the Statue*, what one wish did Pygmalion make to Venus?

08. Who are the <u>five</u> artists of the paintings shown near the bottom of the page? (Click on each "thumbnail" to see a larger image and more information.)

09. In Gerome's *Pygmalion and Galatea* [image 2], is Galatea shown as ivory or as human flesh, or both? Which part of the statue is still stone?

10. How has Paul Delvaux [image 5] changed the story in his version of *Pygmalion*?

BERNARD SHAW'S *PYGMALION*
http://www.bartleby.com/138/

11. How does Professor Henry Higgins reflect the myth of Pygmalion as told in Ovid's *Metamorphoses*?

12. What famous musical, both a Broadway play and a film, was based on Shaw's *Pygmalion?*

13. [*Click on "SEQUEL: WHAT HAPPENED AFTERWARDS*] According to Shaw, why would Eliza Doolittle not marry Professor Higgins and be happy ever after?

THE "PYGMALION PHENOMENON"
http://www.ntlf.com/html/pi/9902/pygm_1.htm

14. What is meant by the "Pygmalion Phenomenon" in the classroom?

HADRIAN'S PANTHEON
http://harpy.uccs.edu/roman/html/hadrian2.html

14. Why was Hadrian called "The Greekling"?

15. To whom was the Pantheon dedicated?

16. How does the height of the Pantheon compare to that of St. Peter's or Chartres Cathedral?

17. Why is the hemispheric dome of the Pantheon important in the history of architecture?

18. Why was much of the bronze used in the Pantheon removed in the 1600s?

TRAJAN'S COLUMN
http://nis-www.lanl.gov/~ctr/trajan_column.html

19. What is the subject of the reliefs depicted on Trajan's column?

20. Whose statue stands at the top of Trajan's Column?

21. The base of the Column is a massive cube containing a number of small rooms. What was the innermost room designed to hold?

22. Who is shown addressing his troops [*see the third image on the page*]?

5. *ANCIENT CIVILIZATIONS OF INDIA AND CHINA*

Study Questions:

INDIAN CIVILIZATION

01. What were the two earliest important urban centers of the Indus River Valley civilization?

02. What is the meaning of the initials "B.C.E."?

03. The invasion of what people around 1500 B.C.E. contributed to the decline of the Indus River civilization?

04. What language was spoken by the Aryans?

05. What were the four major orders of society identified in the Aryan caste system?

06. What term was applied to those who were not members of these four orders?

07. What two great epic poems in India are the equivalent to Homer's *Iliad* and *Odyssey* in Greece and Vergil's *Aeneid* in Rome?

08. What are the oldest religious texts (compiled around 1000 B.C.E.) in India?

09. What is the meaning of the word *Upanishads*?

10. According to the *Upanishads*, what name is given to the impersonal reality that is the ultimate reality?

11. What is the meaning of *Atman* and the significance of the phrase *Tat tvam asi* ("That are thou")?

12. According to the text, "The fundamental aim of Hinduism is to be liberated from the illusory world of empirical reality and to be absorbed into the one true reality called _______________."

13. In Hinduism, what are three paths to achieving an understanding of true reality?

    - __________ the path of ascetism (fasting, nonpossession, body discipline)

    - __________ the path of performing one's duty according to one's caste

    - __________ the path of performing all deeds as an act of devotion

14. What is the meaning of the title *Buddha*?

15. What caused Siddhartha Gautama to wonder about suffering?

16. What is the significance in the life of the Buddha of the Deer Park at Sarnath (near what is now present Benares, or Varanasi)?

17. The "Middle Path," preached by the Buddha in his first sermon, lay between what two extremes?

18. According to the Buddha's Fourfold Noble Truths (the Four Noble Truths),

    a. what is existence?

    b. what causes the suffering of existence?

    c. what is the cessation of suffering called?

    d. what is the fourth path (or truth) to *nirvana*?

19. What is *ahimsa*?

20. According to the Buddha, from where does Truth come?

21. Which Indian emperor unified all of India (including Afghanistan and Baluchistan)?

22. What was Ashoka's view of *ahimsa*?

23. Who first established Buddhism as the religion of the state of India?

24. What were the two purposes of the *stupas* erected by Ashoka? What was the purpose of the stone pillars erected by Ashoka?

25. What was the purpose of the vast Buddhist convocation called together by Ashoka?

26. What was the influence of Ashoka on the spread of Buddhism beyond India?

27. Is Buddhism still the majority religion of India today? Why or why not?

28. With the reign of what emperor did a tradition of large-scale sculpture and architecture appear?

29. What is the subject of the earliest monumental Indian sculpture, 242-232 B.C.E. (figure 5.2)?

30. What is unusual about the subject of the scenes shown from the sculptured frieze on the temple at Khajuraho in northern India (figure 5.3)?

31. What are Buddhist *Bodhisattvas*?

32. After his death, what happened to the empire of Ashoka?

33. What empire was founded by Chandra Gupta I in C.E. 320?

34. Who was the greatest ruler (C.E. c. 380 – c. 415) of the Gupta Empire?

35. During the Gupta period, which religion witnessed a powerful growth, and which religion saw a rapid decline of influence?

36. Who was the most famous Indian Classical writer (active c. C.E. 400) of the Gupta period? What play was his best-known work?

37. From what country did Arabic numbers originate?

38. Around C.E. 480 – 500, what was the influence of the White Huns on the Gupta Empire?

39. What was the religion of the new Indian empire that developed in the fifteenth and sixteenth centuries?

CHINESE CIVILIZATION

40. What was the name of the earliest civilization (c. 1600 – 1100 B.C.E.) in China?

41. What dynasty ruled China from c. 1100 – c. 221 B.C.E.?

42. What were the two chief schools of Chinese philosophy?

43. What role was played by traditional religion in the teachings of Confucius?

44. According to Confucius, what is owed to parents, ancestors, elders, and rulers? Why?

45. In Taoism, what is meant by the *tao*?

46. Who was the traditional founder of Taoism? What book contains the essential teachings of Taoism?

47. According to Taoism, what should humans do to change the world?

48. Does the flow of water change the world?

49. What was the influence of Shih Huang-ti on the government of China? What dynasty (221 – 210 B.C.E.) was established by Shih Huang-ti?

50. What influence did Shih Huang-ti have on philosophical books in China?

51. What did Shih Huang-ti build to defend China against external invaders?

52. What great building project of Shih Huang-ti was rediscovered in 1974 (Fig. 5.11)?

53. What new dynasty ruled China from 202 B.C.E. to C.E. 220?

54. What dynasty (C.E. 618 – 906) ruled during the period of cultural achievement known as China's "Golden Age"?

55. During the Han Dynasty, what religion was introduced from India into China?

56. What is one difference between the two main strains of Buddhism (*Mahayana* Buddhism and *Hinayana* Buddhism)?

57. Who was the most important poet of the T'ang Dynasty (and perhaps the best known of all Chinese poets)?

Thought Questions:

A. Should Hinduism be seen as a form of monotheism because of its belief in Brahman (the one true reality, but with many manifestations)?

B. Do you think Confucianism is a philosophy or a religion? What is the difference between a philosophy and a religion?

C. Taoism teaches the importance of "doing nothing." Can you think of any examples of changing things by "doing nothing"?

D. What is a person supposed to think about while meditating?

What you do not want done to yourself, do not do to others.
– Confucius (c. 551 – 479 B.C.E.)

Define or Identify:

INDIAN CIVILIZATION
- Indus River Valley Civilization - Harappa, Mohenjo-Daro
- Aryans
  - Sanskrit
  - Caste System, Outcastes
  - Epics
    - *Ramayana* – oldest Hindu epic
    - *Mahabharata* – longest Indian epic (100,000 verses)
      - *Baghavad-Gita* – best known part of *Mahabharata*
  - Religious Texts
    - *Vedas, Rig Veda*
    - *Upanishads*
- Hinduism
  - *Brahman*
  - *Atman* ("That are Thou")
  - Yoga
  - *Karma* – "action" and its consequences on future lives
  - [*Dharma* – duties and responsibilities, according to one's position]
  - [*Samsara* – endless cycle of birth, death, and reincarnation]
- Buddhism
  - Siddhartha Gautama
    - The Buddha
    - The Four Noble Truths
    - *Nirvana* – "extinction" of desire, suffering, and ego
    - *Ahimsa* – nonviolence
  - Hinayana / Mahayana Buddhism
- Ashoka
- *Stupas*
- Gupta Empire
  - Chandra Gupta II
  - Kalidasa, *Sakuntala*

CHINESE CIVILIZATION
- Shang Dynasty, c. 1600 – 1100 B.C.E.
- Chou Dynasty, c. 1100 – 221 B.C.E.
- Chinese Philosophy
  - Confucius / King Fu-tse
  - Lao-tzu / Laozi
    - Taoism / Daoism, *Tao te ching / Tao De Jing*
- Ch'in / Qin Dynasty
  - Shih Huang-ti – Great Wall of China; "Burning of the Books"
- Han Dynasty, 202 B.C.E. – C.E. 220
- T'ang Dynasty, 618 – 906—China's "Golden Age"
  - *Five Classics*

CHAPTER 5 - REVIEW

Begin by writing the title of the chapter you've just studied. Next, without looking at the text or your study guide, use your memory to recall and to list the major sections or topics covered in the chapter. Finally, check your knowledge by taking the short "Self Quiz" below.

A) CHAPTER TITLE:

B) MAJOR SECTIONS OR TOPICS:

C) SELF QUIZ # 5 – IDENTIFY THE:

01. ________________ Invaders who introduced both Sanskrit and Hinduism to India.

02. ________________ Oldest religious texts in India (compiled around 1000 B.C.E.)

03. ________________ Philosophy and religion associated with the enlightenment of Siddhartha Gautama.

04. ________________ Term for the state of being in which there is a cessation of individual suffering.

05. ________________ Meaning of the term *ahimsa*.

06. ________________ Characteristic religious buildings found in Buddhist countries.

07. ________________ Indian emperor responsible for the spread of Buddhism beyond India.

08. ________________ First important Chinese philosopher; his teachings emphasized the importance of respect and loyalty to parents, elders, ancestors, and rulers.

09. ________________ Book of wisdom associated with Lao-tzu.

10. ________________ Dynasty founded by Shih-Huang-ti, first emperor of China.

5. WEB QUESTS - ANCIENT INDIA AND CHINA

VISIT: WHAT DO HINDUS BELIEVE? – Part 1
http://www.bbc.co.uk/worldservice/people/features/world_religions/ram/hinduism1.ram

Listen on Real Audio to the first five minutes of this radio program from the BBC (British Broadcasting Corporation).

A reminder: The Real Player is available free, but you have to be careful. Click on this link: www.real.com and CLICK on the word "FREE." On the next page, CLICK on "Download Free Real Player." Be aware the "Premium Player with Super Pass" is not free.

Be prepared for many free advertisements. OR, try this new site available from NPR's Car Talk: http://www.real.com/freeplayer/?rppr=cartalk.com

01. What can be said clearly and with certainty about what all Hindus believe?

02. What is the common creed of Hinduism?

03. Who is the single founder of Hinduism?

04. What is the one sacred book of Hinduism?

05. How much freedom do Hindus have to choose to believe or to challenge beliefs?

06. What do Hindus believe about the value of other religious faiths as valid paths to salvation?

07. From a Hindu perspective, does being a good Christian also mean that you are a good Hindu? Why?

THE DIAMOND SUTRA, C.E. 868
http://www.bl.uk/collections/treasures/diamond.html

08. What is the importance of the *Diamond Sutra* in the history of printing?

09. What year was it made?

10. *[Click on "Turn the pages of the Diamond Sutra online." On the next screen, "Turning the Pages," click on the caption "Diamond Sutra, then "Click to Start" to see and scroll through the entire book. Click on "Audio" to listen to a brief talk on the Diamond Sutra.]* What is found at the beginning of this scroll book? How was this book printed?

VISIT: LAO TZU, *TAO TE CHING*
http://www.wussu.com/laotzu/
Read the very short chapters listed below.

11. Chapter 1: What are the first two lines of the *Tao Te Ching*?

12. Chapter 11: What is it at the center of a wheel that makes it useful? According to the last line of this chapter, from what comes usefulness?

13. Chapter 22: What is the first line of this chapter? (Can you think of any examples in life where this could be true?)

14. Chapter 29: What can be done to improve the universe?

15. Chapter 37: In what does the "Tao" abide?

16. Chapter 41: How doe the wise student react to the "Tao"? the average student? the foolish student? What is the concluding thought of this paragraph?

17. Chapter 43: What overcomes the hardest thing in the universe? (What is the "softest thing" in the universe?)

18. Chapter 56: Complete these two lines,
    "Those who know do not _________.
    Those who talk do not __________.

19. Which of the above chapters was most meaningful to you? Why?

BUDDHA MIND
http://www.buddhamind.info/
Visit and evaluate the Buddha Mind web site. Be aware that this is an unconventional site, consisting of games, mind games, and activities to keep one asking questions about questions. Note the advice on the site's home page, "LOOK here—anywhere—click on sight." Therefore, do not expect a logical, linear site. If you do, you will be disappointed. Begin by selecting one of the three options:

1) Right Brain—for wisdom, creativity, intuition, spontaneity, and "many pages of muchness."

2) Left Brain—find out about Buddhism, the Buddha, the Four Noble Truths, the Eightfold Path, and all things Buddhist.

3) Shrine Room—for meditation, stillness, tranquility, peace, serenity, and silence.

   A. Which option did you choose? What did you like the <u>most</u> about the option you selected? What did you like <u>least</u> about it?

   B. What did you learn from this web site?

END OF SECTION REVIEW OF ANCIENT CIVILIZATIONS

Match the descriptions below with the correct answers:

______	01.	Acropolis	A.	Oldest cave paintings
______	02.	Aeschylus	B.	Oldest statuette
______	03.	Akhenaton	C.	World's first civilization
______	04.	Alexandria	D.	Ancient Mesopotamian writing
______	05.	Apollo	E.	Mesopotamian stepped pyramid
______	06.	*Aphrodite of Cyrene*	F.	First great epic hero; king of Uruk
______	07.	Aristophanes	G.	"An eye for an eye"
______	08.	Aristotle	H.	First known architect
______	09.	Augustus	I.	Pharaoh advocating monotheism
______	10.	Caryatids	J.	Ancient Egyptian writing
______	11.	Confucius	K.	Greatest city of Minoan civilization
______	12.	Constantinople	L.	Greek city-state
______	13.	Cuneiform	M.	Author of the *Iliad*
______	14.	Dionysus	N.	First known woman poet
______	15.	Doric	O.	Greek nude male statue
______	16.	Epicureanism	P.	Simplest order of Greek architecture
______	17.	Forum	Q.	Order of architecture with volutes
______	18.	Gilgamesh	R.	Greek god of logic, order and reason
______	19.	Hammurabi	S.	Greek god of the emotions & of wine
______	20.	Hellenistic	T.	"excessive pride"
______	21.	Herodotus	U.	First Greek playwright (*Oresteia* trilogy)
______	22.	Hieroglyphics	V.	Author of *Oedipus the King* and *Antigone*
______	23.	Homer	W.	Playwright of comedies, e.g., *Lysistrata*
______	24.	*Hubris*	X.	First Greek historian (*Persian Wars*)
______	25.	Imhotep	Y	Leader during the Golden Age of Greece
______	26.	Ionic	Z.	First objective, scientific historian
______	27.	*Kouros*	AA.	Greek philosopher: "Mankind is the measure"
______	28.	Knossus	BB.	Best known teacher of Plato
______	29.	Lascaux	CC.	Greek philosopher of Ideal Reality
______	30.	*Nirvana*	DD.	Best known student of Plato
______	31.	Pantheon	EE.	Most beautiful building of ancient Athens
______	32.	Parthenon	FF.	Site of the Parthenon
______	33.	Pergamum	GG.	Sculptured female figures as columns
______	34.	Pericles	HH.	Praxiteles' nude female statue
______	35.	Plato	II.	*Canon* of proportion and scale
______	36.	Polis	JJ.	Greek-like civilization after Alexander
______	37.	Polykleitos	KK.	Greatest city of the Hellenistic Age
______	38.	Protagoras	LL.	Wealthiest city of Hellenistic Asia
______	39.	Sappho	MM.	Greco-Roman philosophy emphasizing pleasure
______	40.	Siddhartha Gautama	NN	Greco-Roman philo. emphasizing self control
______	41.	Socrates	OO.	Public meeting place of Rome
______	42.	Sophocles	PP.	First great Emperor of Rome
______	43.	Stoicism	QQ.	Greatest Roman poet; author of *Aeneid*
______	44.	Sumer	RR.	Roman building topped by a dome & oculus
______	45.	*Tao te ching*	SS.	Most important city of Eastern Roman Empire
______	46.	Thucydides	TT.	Year of the fall of Rome
______	47.	Venus of Willendorf	UU.	Teacher of the Four Noble Truths
______	48.	Vergil	VV.	Buddhist extinction of desire and suffering
______	49.	Ziggurats	WW.	Best known Chinese sage
______	50.	476	XX.	Book of wisdom associated with Lao-tse

REVIEW I - B – GEOGRAPHY AND ART: THE ANCIENT WORLD

YOUR ASSIGNMENT:

A) Use the maps in your textbook to identify the locations marked on the map below.

B) Match from the below list the work of art or architecture associated with the place you've identified:

A)	Location on map:	B)	Original Location of work of art:
1. _____	GIZA	_____	Akhenaton & Queen Nefertiti
2. _____	AMARNA	_____	Altar to Zeus
3. _____	UR	_____	Hammurabi's Law Code
4. _____	BABYLON	_____	Palace of Knossus
5. _____	KNOSSUS, CRETE	_____	Pantheon
6. _____	ATHENS	_____	Parthenon
7. _____	PERGAMUM	_____	Sphinx and Pyramids
8. _____	ROME	_____	Ziggurat

6. *JERUSALEM AND EARLY CHRISTIANITY*

Study Questions:

01. What were two of the central sources that led to the development of Western civilization as we know it today?

02. According to the Bible, who was the father (patriarch) of the Hebrews?

03. Who was the leader of the Hebrews in their exodus from Egypt?

04. Who were the three most important kings of the United Monarchy?

05. Who conquered the northern kingdom (Israel) in the eighth century B.C.E.? the southern kingdom (Judah) in 587 B.C.E.?

06. What was the "Babylonian Captivity"?

07. The English word "Bible" comes from the Greek name of what ancient city?

08. What was the original meaning of the word "prophet"?

09. What does the word "canon" mean when applied to the Bible?

10. Compare "monotheism," "henotheism," and "polytheism."

11. What beings were created by God as the apex and crown of nature?

12. What is the Biblical meaning of "covenant"? of "testament"?

13. What is the name of the ethical rules given to Moses after the Exodus but before the Hebrews reached the promised land?

14. What is the difference between a "prophet" and a "seer"?

15. What are the four most important sources of information about Jesus?

16. What was the meaning of the Anglo-Saxon word from which "gospel" comes?

17. What is the meaning of the title "Christ"? of Messiah?

18. What doctrine "became a centerpiece of Christian faith and preaching" and the basis on which early Christianity proclaimed Jesus as Christ?

19. What person became the most important figure in the development and spread of the Christian church after the death of Jesus?

20. Why were early Christians persecuted by the government of Rome?

21. Which emperor in C.E. 312 issued in Milan a decree of toleration for Christianity (and other religions)?

22. What are "frescoes"?

23. What is unusual about the face of Christ in the wall painting [figure 6.3] of *Christ Teaching the Apostles* (c. C.E. 300)?

24. What were three of the early symbols of Christianity?

25. What was the meaning of the Chi-Rho monogram (figure 6.7)?

26. What two famous churches were built during the reign of the Emperor Constantine – in the Vatican (326)? – in Jerusalem (345)?

27. According to the illustration and the floor plan of Old Saint Peter's Basilica, Rome (figures 6.10 and 6.12):

    – What was the basic shape of the basilica?

    – What was the name of its courtyard?

    – What was the name of the central portion, between the side aisles?

    – What was the name of the area intersecting the nave at right angles?

Thought Questions:

A. What is the significance to you of God pronouncing in the Book of Genesis "each part of creation and creation as a whole as 'good,'" compared with the alternative view that the material universe is evil?

B. Do you agree with the view of some that the material world is a gift of God and that therefore human beings are obliged to care for it and be grateful for it?

C. Should the Ten Commandments be publicly displayed in government buildings and classrooms in the United States? Why or why not?

What indeed has Athens to do with Jerusalem? – Tertullian (160 – 230)

Define or Identify:

Monotheism
Henotheism
Polytheism
Patriarch
Abraham
Covenant
Bible: Old and New Testaments
Ten Commandments
canon (in architecture; in literature)
Testament
prophet / seer
disciple

"gospel"
"Christ" / "Messiah"
Resurrection
Paul – spread of Christianity
Mithraism
Constantine, Edict of 312
Chi-Rho monogram (sign)
icon
iconography

basilica
atrium
nave
transept
clerestory
fresco

Significant Works To Recognize and Remember

Ten Commandments
Beatitudes (Sermon on the Mount)
Gospels (Matthew, Mark, Luke, and John)
Christ Teaching the Apostles, C.E. 300
Old St. Peter's Basilica, c. C.E. 333
Church of the Holy Sepulcher, c. C.E. 340

Where there is no vision, the people perish. – Proverbs, 29:18

CHAPTER 6 - REVIEW

Begin by writing the title of the chapter you've just studied. Next, without looking at the text or your study guide, use your memory to recall and to list the major sections or topics covered in the chapter. Finally, check your knowledge by taking the short "Self Quiz" below.

A) CHAPTER TITLE:

B) MAJOR SECTIONS OR TOPICS:

C) SELF QUIZ # 6 – IDENTIFY THE:

01. _______________ Belief in one God.

02. _______________ Word setting out the relationship of God to the Hebrew people ("I will be your God, you will be my people").

03. _______________ Word from the Anglo-Saxon meaning "good news"; the four biblical accounts (Matthew, Mark, Luke and John) of the life of Jesus.

04. _______________ Most important figure in the spread of Christianity into the non-Jewish world of the Roman Empire.

05. _______________ Emperor issuing in C.E. 312 a decree of toleration for Christianity.

06. _______________ Name given to wall paintings done on fresh plaster.

07. _______________ Rectangular building used by early Christians for church services; originally a Roman hall used for public meetings and law courts.

08. _______________ Section of a church intersecting the nave at right angles.

09. _______________ Name of the courtyard preceding the narthex of early churches.

10. _______________ Early symbol of Christianity composed of the first two letters of Christ's name in Greek.

6. WEB QUESTS - JUDAISM AND EARLY CHRISTIANITY

SCROLLS FROM THE DEAD SEA: THE ANCIENT LIBRARY OF QUMRAN AND MODERN SCHOLARSHIP
http://metalab.unc.edu/expo/deadsea.scrolls.exhibit/intro.html
Read the following sections from this exhibit at the Library of Congress:

– "Introduction"
– "Qumran Library"
– "Qumran Community"
– "Today-2000 Years Later "

01. In what year were the scrolls discovered?

02. How many scrolls were at first discovered?

03. How old are the scrolls?

04. Where is Qumran?

05. What three languages are found in the Qumran Library?

06. What is the significance today of the scrolls?

07. What has been the most heated controversy about the scrolls since the 1980s?

ANCIENT MANUSCRIPTS - NEW TESTAMENT
http://www.biblefacts.org/history/oldtext.html

08. What are the names of the two oldest complete Bibles in existence?

09. Why are older manuscripts numbered P1 through P5300?

10. What is the importance of the Rylands Papyrus P52? What is the approximate date of this papyrus? When and where was it discovered? Where is it now?

11. *CLICK on the words* "Rylands Papyrus (P52)" *to answer these questions*: What verses from the Gospel of John are shown? What question has Pilate asked Jesus? Why are some letters shown in red?

12. What is the approximate date for the *Codex Sinaiticus?* [*CLICK on the words "Codex Sinaiticus" at the top of the page.]*

CHRISTIANS IN THE AGE OF PERSECUTIONS
http://www.catacombe.roma.it/en/persecuzioni.html
Please read:

– Introduction. The "IDENTITY CARD" of the Christians.
– From the Letter to Diognetus (apology by unknown author, second century)
– From the "Books to Autolicus" of S. Theophilus of Antioch, second century
– From "The Apologeticus" of Tertullian, second – third century

13. Why were Christians outlawed and persecuted by the Romans? (What accusations were made against Christians?)

14. What edict in 313 ended the persecutions (and the age of martyrs)?

15. What defenses ("apologies") were made by Christians?
– Letter to Diognetus:
– "They dwell on earth, but are _____ _____ _____."
– "They are in the world as the soul is ____ _____ _____."

– "Books to Autolicus:
– "I shall pay homage to the emperor, but I will not _____ _____."

– Apologeticus of Tertullian:
– "You will never find any Christians in prison, unless he be there ____ _______ _______."

CORE RELIGIOUS BELIEFS
VISIT one of the below web sites, and use Real Player to listen to the program of your choice from the BBC (British Broadcasting Corporation) program.

- **JUDAISM: QUESTIONS OF FAITH**
http://www.bbc.co.uk/worldservice/people/features/world_religions/ram/judaism4.ram

- **CHRISTIANITY: THE LIFE OF JESUS CHRIST – WHAT ABOUT THE RESURRECTION?**
http://www.bbc.co.uk/worldservice/people/features/world_religions/ram/christianity3.ram

16. What were the three most important statements you heard on the broadcast?

PIER PAOLO PASOLINI, THE GOSPEL ACCORDING TO ST. MATTHEW (1964)
http://www.gospelcom.net/cgi-bin/ramhurl?f=hollywoodjesus/GAMrichman.rm

17. What are two lessons taught by Jesus (Matthew 19:16-29) shown in this two-minute excerpt from Pasolini's award-winning movie?

7. *BYZANTIUM*

Study Questions:

LATE ROMAN EMPIRE

01. In C.E. 330, what city was dedicated by the emperor Constantine as the eastern capital of the Roman Empire?

02. What was the original Greek name for Constantinople?

03. From 402 to 476, what city served as the western capital of the Roman Empire?

04. Which two important writers witnessed the decline of the West (one from the city of Ravenna, the other from Hippo in Roman north Africa)? Which one is generally considered to be the greatest writer of the early Christian West?

05. In *The City of God*, what was Augustine's explanation for the Visigoth sacking of Rome in 410? (What group did many Romans blame for the event?)

06. What was Augustine's concept of "human nature"? How did his view compare with that of Paul? of John Calvin?

07. What was Augustine's view of history: linear or cyclical?

08. What work of Augustine's is considered the beginning of self-reflective autobiography in the West?

09. Who was the most important author in Ravenna in the twilight period between the last Roman emperor and the arrival of Justinian's troops?

10. What book was written by Boethius, and what was its message?

BYZANTIUM

11. What city was the center of imperial life in the Roman Empire in the early fifth century?

12. What were the most important achievements of Justinian:

    – legal?   – architectural?

13. What does it mean to codify law?

14. Why did Justinian close the last surviving Platonic academy?

15. What was the principal church ("Holy Wisdom") of Justinian's Constantinople?

16. What are "pendentives"? How were they used to combine a dome with a basilica?

17. What name is given to the order of sequences of the various parts of a worship service?

18. In what year did Constantinople fall to the Turks? To what use was Hagia Sophia converted after 1453? What is it used for today?

RAVENNA

19. For what type of art is the Mausoleum of Galla Placidia famous?

20. What was unusual about the portrayal of Christ in the mosaic of *The Good Shepherd* (from the fifth-century mausoleum of Galla Placidia in the city of Ravenna)?

21. What is the name of the small pieces of stone used to make a mosaic?

22. What are the four books in the open cabinet on the left side of the mosaic of *The Martyrdom of Saint Lawrence* (from the mausoleum of Galla Placidia in Ravenna)?

23. What is the name for the eastern end of a church, often semicircular, where the altar is found?

24. How does the shape of the Church of San Vitale in Ravenna differ from traditional basilica design?

25. Which church in Ravenna provided the inspiration for Charlemagne's church at Aachen (Aix-la-Chapelle)?

26. What word, from the Greek meaning "one who rules or dominates all," is often used for the figure of God or Christ found in the apse of Byzantine churches?

27. What is the meaning of the chi and rho signs found on the famous wall mosaics of San Vitale, Ravenna?

28. In the ceiling mosaic of Christ enthroned in San Vitale, Ravenna (Christ the Pantocrator [figure 7.16]),

    – is Christ shown with or without a beard?

    – How do we know it is Saint Vitalis at the far left?

    – What is Bishop Ecclesius (at the extreme right) holding in his hands?

29. What was the purpose of the bishops' *cathedra*? What is the difference between a church and a cathedral?

30. What was the importance of the *Codex Sinaiticus* discovered in Saint Catherine's monastery at Mount Sinai? Where is it now displayed?

31. What is the meaning of the term "codex"? [See Key Terms at the end of the chapter.]

32. What is the meaning of the Greek word "icon"? [What is an "iconoclast"?]

33. In the Byzantine world, what images of art served as "windows into the world of the sacred"?

34. What influence did the religious services held in Hagia Sophia have on Prince Vladimir of Russia?

Thought Questions:

A. Should Justinian have been more tolerant of "pagan" learning?

B. What is "pagan" learning?

C. If history is cyclical, when does it begin? When does it end? If history is linear, when does it begin? When does it end (with what event)?

Unless you believe, you will not understand. – Saint Augustine (C.E. 354 – 430)

Define or Identify:

Augustine of Hippo
Confessions (autobiography), 397
The City of God (linear history), 413 – 426

Ravenna
Boethius, *The Consolation of Philosophy,* c. 522 – 524

Constantinople
Justinian, 527-565
The Code
Hagia Sophia / Aya Sophia

liturgy
mosaics
tesserae
icon
cathedra
codex

Significant Works To Recognize and Remember

Hagia Sophia / Aya Sophia (Holy Wisdom), Constantinople, 532 – 537
The Good Shepherd, Mausoleum of Galla Placidia, Ravenna, c. 450
Church of San Vitale, Ravenna, c. 526 – 547
Emperor Justinian and Courtiers (wall mosaic)
Empress *Theodora and Retinue* (wall mosaic)
Codex Sinaiticus (oldest Greek manuscript of New Testament), c. 350

CHAPTER 7 - REVIEW

Begin by writing the title of the chapter you've just studied. Next, without looking at the text or your study guide, use your memory to recall and to list the major sections or topics covered in the chapter. Finally, check your knowledge by taking the short "Self Quiz" below.

A) CHAPTER TITLE:

B) MAJOR SECTIONS OR TOPICS:

C) SELF QUIZ # 7 – IDENTIFY THE:

01. ________________ Capital city of the Byzantine Empire.

02. ________________ Book by Augustine rejecting earlier cyclical views and setting forth a linear view of history.

03. ________________ Autobiographical book by Augustine written so "I would know myself that I might know thee [God]".

04. ________________ Author of *The Consolation of Philosophy*; written while imprisoned in Ravenna by Theodoric the Ostrogoth.

05. ________________ Earliest manuscript in Greek of the New Testament; found in Saint Catherine's monastery at Mt. Sinai.

06. ________________ Principal church of Constantinople ("Holy Wisdom").

07. ________________ Type of art consisting of small pieces of stone or glass set into plaster or cement.

08. ________________ Capital City of the Roman Empire in the west from 402 to 476; location of the Church of San Vitale.

09. ________________ Images of art, which in the Byzantine world, served as "windows into the world of the sacred."

10. ________________ Year in which Constantinople was conquered by the Turks and the Byzantine Empire ended.

11. ________________ Book with bound pages (instead of a scroll)

7. WEB QUESTS - BYZANTIUM

HAGIA SOPHIA / AYA SOFIA
http://www.patriarchate.org/ecumenical_patriarchate/chapter_4/html/hagia_sophia.html

01. What is the subject of the first visual displayed on this page?

02. In two words, what does the name Hagia Sophia mean? In four words?

03. How many years did it take to build Hagia Sophia?

04. What was the fate of the Hagia Sophia on Tuesday, May 29,1453, at the hands of Sultan Mehmet the Conqueror?

A BRIEF GUIDE TO BYZANTINE ICONS
http://home.earthlink.net/~zoemark/icon.htm

05. What was the meaning of the Greek word *eikona* (from which comes the English word "icon")?

06. What are four subjects ordinarily depicted in icons?

07. (Scroll down to "A Short History of the Icon.) What does the second Commandment say about the making of images?

08. How does the author of this web page justify the creation of icons?

09. (Scroll down to "The Icon of Christ.) Compare in this section the two icons of Christ.

    a) What is the difference in appearance of the book carried in Christ's right hand? Which of these two icons is titled "Christ the Teacher? Why?

    b) What is used to illustrate Divine Light emanating from within a person?

    c) From what monastery is the first icon, *Christ the Ruler of All (Pantocrator)*?

SAINT CATHERINE'S MONASTERY AT MOUNT SINAI
http://interoz.com/egypt/Catherines.htm

10. Between C.E. 527 and 565, what Roman Emperor ordered the construction of St. Catherine's Monastery?

11. What is important about its collection of illuminated manuscripts? (Where in the world is the largest collection of illuminated manuscripts?)

12. Around the year 1850, what fourth-century manuscript was discovered in the St. Catherine's monastery?

CODEX SINAITICUS
http://divinity.mcmaster.ca/OpenText/resources/articles/a1

13. Why is the *Codex Sinaiticus* important in the study of the New Testament?

14. Which text is more complete, the *Codex Sinaiticus* or the *Codex Vaticanus*?

SYMBOLS IN CHRISTIAN ART AND ARCHITECTURE
http://home.att.net/~wegast/symbols/crosses/crosses.htm

15. Draw a sketch of the below Christian crosses:

a) Baptismal Cross
b) Byzantine Cross
c) Calvary (Graded) Cross
d) Celtic (Irish) Cross
e) Eastern (Russian) Cross
f) Greek Cross
g) Latin Cross
h) Maltese Cross
i) Papal Cross
k) Patriarchal Cross
l) St. Andrew's Cross
m) Triumphant Cross with Orb

8. ISLAM

Study Questions:

01. Who is considered the founder of Islam? When and where was he born? When did he begin speaking publicly about his ideas of religious reform (at about the age of forty)?

02. What event in 622 marks the beginning of the Islamic calendar?

03. What was the significance of the Qa'aba?

04. What is the meaning of the word "Islam"?

05. How does the Islamic concept of monotheism compare with the Christian doctrine of the Trinity?

06. What are the five pillars of Islam?

    a. to believe and recite that there is _____ God.

    b. to pray _____ times each day facing ________.

    c. to donate ______________________________.

    d. to _____ during the holy month of ____________.

    e. to make a ___________ to Mecca.

07. What are teachings of Islam regarding

    a. the eating of pork?

    b. the consumption of alcoholic beverages?

    c. polygamy?

08. What is the holy book of Islam? How is the book organized?

09. What is the language of the *Koran* (*Quran*)? Why is it taught the *Koran* (*Quran*)? should not be translated from the Arabic?

10. What is the name of the body of literature which consists of authoritative commentaries on the *Koran/ Quran*) and explanations of oral traditions?

11. What word comes from the two Greek words that mean "beautiful writing"?

12. What is the name of the most important book in Arabic to which the skills of calligraphy are applied?

13. What is the name of the place of worship in Islamic communities?

14. Why are mosques decorated with abstract art and calligraphy rather than pictorial representations?

15. Which day of the week is the special day of prayer in Islam?

16. What is the purpose of the niche in the wall (*mihrab*) of the mosque?

17. What is the purpose of the minaret or minarets adjacent to the mosque?

18. What building in Jerusalem is one of the earliest and most spectacular achievements of Islamic architecture?

19. How many sides are there to the octagonal Dome of the Rock? What color is its dome?

20. In what century did Muslims arrive in Spain? What city became the Muslim capital in Spain?

21. What was the goal of the *Reconquista*?

22. In what year was the *Reconquista* successful and Muslims were forced out of Spain by Christians?

23. What was the name of the palace complex in Granada that escaped destruction during the *Reconquista*?

24. What was the most beautiful and most famous example of Islamic architecture in Muslim India during the time of the Mughal emperors?

25. What was the original purpose of the Taj Mahal? The Taj Mahal is located in what city of India?

26. Which is the name of the most mystical branch or tradition of Islam?

27. What is the role of the *sheyks* of Sufism?

28. What is the goal of the practices and disciplines of Sufism?

29. Which thirteenth-century writer is the most famous of the Sufi mystics?

30. What language did the Sufi mystic Rumi (1207 – 1273) use in writing his religious verse?

31. What was distinctive about the way Rumi recited his poetry? What did Rumi believe to be the purpose of combining recitation with dance?

32. What city was the political and cultural capital of the Abbasid Dynasty?

33. What was the influence on the works of Aristotle of scholars working in Baghdad's "House of Wisdom" (*Bait-al-hikma)?*

34. What was the influence of Al-Khwarizmi (780 – 850), the greatest scholar at Baghdad's "House of Wisdom" on:

    – Algebra?

    – Arabic numerals?

35. From what civilization came the symbols used by Al-Khwarizmi in developing Arabic numerals?

36. From what civilization came such words as orange, lemon, sugar, alcohol, and sherbert?

37. What did *The Incoherence of the Philosophers* by Al-Ghazali (d. 1111) have to say about Greek philosophy?

38. What was the response of Averröes (d. 1198) in his book *The Incoherence of Incoherence* about the issue of reconciling Greek philosophy with Islam?

Thought Questions:

A. The Islamic creed consists of the single sentence, *La ilaha illa Allah; Muhammad rasul Allah*. Which do you think is a more accurate translation: "There is no God but Allah; Muhammad is the messenger of Allah" or "There is no God but God; Muhammad is the messenger of God"? Why?

B. Is the *Allah* of Islam the same God as the Judeo-Christian God?

C. What are the similarities and differences between the *jihad* of Islam and the crusade of Christianity?

Define or Identify:

Mecca
- Qa'aba

Medina
Muhammad (570 – 632)
Islam ("submission")
Koran / Quran (revelations or recitations)
- Five Pillars of Faith

calligraphy
mosque
- Mihrab
- Minaret

Islamic architecture
- Dome of the Rock, Jerusalem, late 600s
- Córdoba Mosque, Spain, mid 900s
- Alhambra Palace, Granada, Spain, 1354 – 1391
- Taj Mahal, Agra, India, 1631 – 1647

Reconquista

Sufi
- Rumi (1207 – 1273)

Baghdad, Abbasid Dynasty
- "House of Wisdom"
  - Al-Khwarizmi (780 – 850)
    - Algebra
    - "Arabic" numbers
- Averröes, *The Incoherence of Incoherence*

Other Important Works (Not in the textbook)

Rubaiyat of Omar Khayyam
Thousand and One Nights / The Arabian Nights

The Moving Finger writes; and, having writ,
Moves on: nor all your Piety nor Wit
Shall lure it back to cancel half a Line,
Nor all your Tears wash out a Word of it.
– Omar Khayyam, *The Rubaiyat*

CHAPTER 8 - REVIEW

Begin by writing the title of the chapter you've just studied. Next, without looking at the text or your study guide, use your memory to recall and to list the major sections or topics covered in the chapter. Finally, check your knowledge by taking the short "Self Quiz" below.

A) CHAPTER TITLE:

B) MAJOR SECTIONS OR TOPICS:

C) SELF QUIZ # 8 – IDENTIFY THE:

01. ________________ Arabic word for God.

02. ________________ Religion and way of life based on the revelations received by Muhammad; the word means "submission" to God.

03. ________________ Sacred book of Islam.

04. ________________ Muhammad's emigration with his followers from Mecca to Medina in 622; considered year one of the Muslim calendar.

05. ________________ Building used as a Muslim place of worship.

06. ________________ Special day of the week for prayer by Muslims.

07. ________________ Attractive writing found in Muslim sacred books and on Muslim buildings; it comes from two Greek words meaning "beautiful writing."

08. ________________ City of "House of Wisdom," of the Abbasid Dynasty; place of preservation and translation of Greek manuscripts. including the works of Aristotle

09. ________________ Beautiful Muslim palace complex in Granada, Spain.

10. ________________ The year the *Reconquista* was successful and the last Muslims left Spain.

11. ________________ The most beautiful and most famous example of Islamic architecture in Muslim India during the time of the Mughal emperors.

8. WEB QUESTS - ISLAM

ISLAM – EMPIRE OF FAITH – GOD VS ALLAH
http://www.pbs.org/empires/islam/faithgod.html

01. What is the difference between God and *Allah*?

02. What is the difference between God, *Dieu*, and *Gott*?

ISLAM – EMPIRE OF FAITH – ISLAM TODAY
http://www.pbs.org/empires/islam/faithtoday.html

03. What are the two main branches of Islam?

04. What issue or question caused a split in Islam?

05. Which group accepted the succession of Muhammad's elected successors, who were known as caliphs?

06. What was the original meaning of the word *Sunni*? of *Shiite*?

07. Which group believed that any head of the community had to be a direct descendant of Muhammad through his daughter Fatima and her husband Ali?

08. To which group do the vast majority of Muslims belong today?

ISLAMIC ART BY ELIZABETH SIDDIQUI
http://www.colostate.edu/Orgs/MSA/find_more/islart.html

09. According to the author, "art is the _______ of a culture and its world view."

10. What is the Arabic word for God?

11. Thought Question: In your opinion, is *Allah* (the God of Islam) the same God as of Judaism and Christianity? Why?

12. Why has Islamic art developed a unique character using a number of primary forms (geometric, arabesque, floral, and calligraphic)?

13. Why are the typical subjects of western art not included (indeed they are prohibited) from Islamic art?

14. What do the intricate systems of interconnected geometric forms say about the Islamic view of Allah and the Cosmos?

15. Define "calligraphy."

16. Why is calligraphy an important form of art in Islam?

17. According to the Prophet of Islam some 1400 years ago, "God is Beautiful and Loves ________."

18. Said the same prophet, "God likes that when you do anything, you do ___ _____."

OMAR KHAYYAM, THE RUBAIYAT
http://tehran.stanford.edu/Literature/Poetry/Omar_Khayyam.html
[This URL is case-sensitive; be sure to type capital letters as capitals.]

19. Read the following verses and answer the below questions.

– Verse 11: What four things can provide happiness ("Paradise enow")?

– Verses 17, 18, 22, and 23: What is the fate of Jamshyd, Bahram, Caesar (and us)?

– Verses 42 and 43: What can change "Life's leaden Metal into Gold"?

– Verse 49: How many choices do humans have? Why?

– Verse 51: What is the meaning of "The Moving Finger writes; and, having writ, Moves on"?

– Verses 52 and 71: Does it appear that Omar Khayyam was a good Muslim? Why?

20. In one sentence, what you think Omar Khayyam was saying to us?

SUFISM
http://www.zenzibar.com/Articles/ed-2-6.htm

21. What name is given to the branch of Islam that emphasizes mysticism?

22. All Muslims believe that it is possible to become close to God after death and judgment. The Sufis believe, like most mystical groups, that this is possible _________ ________.

23. Sufi Stories **http://www.inspirationalstories.com/sufism-1.html**

24. What is the meaning of each of these three Sufi stories?

    a. "Nasrudin Steals the Happiness"

    b. "Priorities"

    c. "Desire"

ISLAM: THE QUR'AN - THE PATH ILLUMINATED
http://www.bbc.co.uk/worldservice/people/features/world_religions/ram/islam1.ram
Listen to this BBC (British Broadcasting Corporation) program and take notes on its content. This site requires the use of Real Audio Player.

25. What are the five most important statements you heard on this program?

a)

b)

c)

d)

e)

9. *CHARLEMAGNE AND THE RISE OF MEDIEVAL CULTURE*

Study Questions:

CHARLEMAGNE

01. In C.E. 800 on Christmas Day, what significant event took place in Saint Peter's Basilica in Rome?

02. How far did Charlemagne's kingdom extend to the south? to the north? to the east?

03. What was the importance of the victory of Charles Martel and the Franks at Poitiers (Tours?) in 732?

04. Who were the opposing sides in the Battle of Roncesvalles (778)? What epic was inspired by this battle?

05. What was the relationship of Charlemagne's "palace school" at Aachen to the Carolingian Renaissance?

06. Who was the most important scholar (an Anglo-Saxon) at Aachen?

07. What important English monk influenced Alcuin of York [this monk is also remembered for his *Ecclesiastical History of the English People*, 731, in which he dated all events as either BC and AD]?

08. What was the name for the medieval course of study that included grammar, rhetoric, and logic? the course of study that included arithmetic, geometry, music, and astronomy?

09. What was the goal of dialectics?

MONASTICISM

10. What is the meaning of the Greek word *monos*? How does the meaning of *monos* clarify for us the meaning of the word monasticism?

11. What is "asceticism"? "eremitism"?

12. Who was the author of the most famous "Rule" in western monasticism?

13. What important monastery in Italy was founded by Saint Benedict? What were the important requirements of the monastic life as set forth by him?

14. Why did Benedictine monks take a vow of poverty? of stability? of obedience? of remaining unmarried (chastity)?

15. What was the Benedictine motto? (__________ & __________)

16. According to the Benedictine *horarium*, what time of day did monks arise? What happened after the *None* (ninth hour)? When did they go to bed?

17. In a typical day, how many hours did Benedictine monks spend at prayer? at reading? at work?

18. What word (meaning "things read aloud") was used for the reading aloud in churches of the lives of the saints?

MUSIC, DRAMA, AND LITERATURE

19. What type of chant became the predominant type of music in Roman Catholic churches during the early middle ages?

20. What does it mean to say that Gregorian chants were sung *a capella*?

21. What was the influence on western drama of the addition of words (*tropes*) to the extensive elaboration of the final syllable (*melisma*) of a Gregorian chant?

22. What is the importance of the *Quem Queritis* trope?

23. Why can early medieval drama be described as "liturgical drama"?

24. What were the subjects of the fourteenth-century cycle of plays underwritten by craft or merchant guilds?

25. What was the purpose of the fifteenth-century play *Everyman*?

26. What is the meaning of the term *memento mori*? Why is the motif of *Everyman* a good example of a *memento mori*?

27. How important was "will" for the salvation of *Everyman*?
Do you think that "will" (including the willingness to learn) is important?

28. Around the year 1,000, what German nun and poet wrote non-liturgical plays such as *Theophilus* and *The Conversion of the Harlot Thais*?

29. What is the importance of *Theophilus* in the history of the Faust legend? What is the lesson of Faust for those of us who live in a materialistic society?

30. What was the primary purpose of a "reliquary"? (See figure 9.3)

31. What is the oldest and most famous *chanson de geste* or *chanson d'histoire*?

32. What eighth-century ruler of the Franks was celebrated in the eleventh-century *Song of Roland*?

33. Whose shrine at Santiago de Compostela in Spain became a major pilgrimage site?

34. Who were the *jongleurs*, and how did they spread the *Song of Roland*? In Italy, what name was given to Roland?

ILLUMINATED BOOKS

35. What was "parchment," and why was it the principal material for writing in the middle ages?

36. What is an "illuminated" book (or manuscript)?

37. What illuminated book (now at the University of Utrecht in Holland) is considered the literary masterpiece of the Carolingian Renaissance?

38. How was ivory used to decorate medieval books?

39. In the ivory carving of the *Crucifixion (*figure 9.6),

    – what scene in the life of Christ is depicted in the:

        – lower left corner?

        – the scene directly above?

    – what is the soldier on the left doing? on the right?

    – in the upper left corner, whose hand is helping Jesus ascend into heaven?

    – is Jesus shown clean shaven or with a beard?

40. In the *Dagulf Psalter* (figure 9.7), what is unusual about the initial letter of the first, fifty-first, and hundred-first psalms?

41. What was distinctive about Carolingian books, specifically the material used for pages? covers? illuminating?

42. What was "Carolingian minuscule"? Why was it important? How did it compare with "majuscule"?

ARCHITECTURE

43. In what town did Charlemagne build his palace and royal chapel? What was the French name for this town?

Define or Identify:

Battle of Poitiers, 732 (F
Charlemagne (Charles t
Aachen / Aix-la-C
Carolingian Rena
Palace Sc
Trivium /
Carolingia
Coronation as Er

Gregorian Chant
monophonic
a capella
melisma
tropes
asceticism
monasticism
St. Benedict
Hildegard of Bingen
"legends" (things read al
scriptorium
Illuminated manuscripts
memento mori
Romanesque architectur
Al Andalus / Spain
Reconquista
Arabs and Aristot

Significant Works To R

Rule of St. Benedict
Utrecht Psalter
Song of Roland (Orlando
Quem Queritas trope
Everyman (Morality play

Other Important Works (Not

Lindisfarne Gospels, c. 7
Beowulf, early 700s
Book of Kells, c. 800
Bayeux Tapestry, 1066 -

44. What was the basic Charlemagne's visi design for his royal most important relic the words "cape" ar

45. In monasteries, wh

– chapter house

– cloister?

46. What was the name and 1150?

47. What were two cha

48. Were Romanesque

49. What was the prima

50. Why did Bernard of churches?

Thought Questions:

A. Medieval scholars e Which of your colleg

B. Legends ("things re middle ages. Do w examples for us? Do or the weaknesses o

C. Who is your hero or like to be more alike

D. Can we serve as a h

E. Bernard of Clairvaux Do you prefer churc decorated? Why?

Idleness is the enemy of th be occupied in manual lab

Image 14

n. To whom is Harold now speaking (shown at the far left of the panel?

o. What building in shown in the center of this panel?
Thought Question: What do you think is the significance of God's hand pointing towards the building?

p. Whose body is being carried into the building? What are the words at the top of this panel?

Image 15

q. At the far left, who is shown speaking his last words, and then (below), "DEFUNCTUS EST"?

r. In this scene, what two objects are being offered to Harold? (What do you think *corona* means?)

s. How do we know Harold has become king? (What do you think "HAROLD REX : ANGLORUM" means?

Image 16

t. What news do you think is being carried aboard the ship? At the far right, what orders are being issued by Duke William?

View Images 17 to 33 in order to see the Battle of Hastings in C.E. 1066.

Image 34

u. Who is shown being cut down by a mounted Norman knight?

v. What act is shown in the final scene depicted in the Bayeux Tapestry?

INTRODUCTION TO MEDIEVAL HISTORY - THE BAYEUX TAPESTRY
http://www.ku.edu/kansas/medieval/108/lectures/bayeux_tapestry.html

02. What did you learn from reading the below paragraphs of this essay?

a. Paragraph 2:

b. Paragraph 4:

c. Paragraph 5:

d. Paragraph 6:

10. HIGH MIDDLE AGES: THE SEARCH FOR SYNTHESIS

Study Questions:

GOTHIC CATHEDRALS

01. From c. 1150 to 1300, what city was the intellectual and cultural center of Western civilization?

02. What was the contribution of the Abbot Suger and the Abbey of St. Denis to Gothic architecture?

03. What is the name of the part of the church

    – one enters first (before the nave)?

    – where monks sang the Office?

    – behind the high altar (with an aisle around the apse)?

04. What city was at the center of the Île de France?

05. What were the two major characteristics of Gothic architecture?

06. What made possible the increased height of Gothic cathedrals?

07. What is meant by "Gothic luminosity"?

08. How did Gothic architecture allow more of the "light of God" into the cathedral?

09. Which medieval cathedral (southwest of Paris) is famous for its 173 stained glass windows, including the "Notre Dame de Belle Verriere"? (What was the subject of the stained glass window "Notre Dame de Belle Verriere"?)

10. What was the specific reason why La Sainte Chapelle was built?

11. What is the most striking aspect of its upper chapel (figure 10.4)?

12. What parts of the medieval cathedral served as a "Bible in Stone" for the illiterate?

13. What was the functional purpose of the Gothic gargoyles?
    What was their didactic function?

14. In the tympanum from Chartres (shown in figure 10.6),

    – who is shown in the center seated in majesty?

- where is the baby Jesus?
- who do you think is the man standing to the left?
- what is the occupation of the two men to the right?

15. What was the purpose of the "signature frames" found at the bottom of many stained-glass windows?

MEDIEVAL SCHOLARS AND SAINTS

16. In the illustration (figure 10.12) from the Lecture of Henricus de Alemania (Henry of Germany),
    - What is the lecturer reading from that sits atop the lectern?
    - Do you think his book is written by hand or is printed? Why?
    - How many students are in the classroom?
    - How many students are paying full attention?
    - How many are asleep, daydreaming, or talking to each other?
17. Which are the three oldest universities in Europe?
18. What three degrees were awarded by medieval universities?
19. What "new learning" was re-introduced to western Europe from Muslim sources in Spain?

20 How did the location of cathedral schools differ from that of the monastic schools?

21. Which was the most famous and representative university of the Middle Ages? Why was it famous?
22. Who was the most famous teacher at the University of Paris in the early 1100s?

23 What was the subject of Peter Abelard's *Sic et Non*?

24. What was the original meaning of the term *universitas*?
25. Who organized and controlled the *universitas* at Paris? at Bologna?
26. What was a student qualified to do with a master of arts degree?
27. In what three areas could a medieval holder of the M.A. receive a doctorate?

28. What was the origin of the name "Latin Quarter"?

29. By the end of the twelfth century, what city was the intellectual center of western Europe?

30. What action in 1258 resulted in the origin of the Sorbonne?

31. In a student's day at the University of Paris,

    – at what time was the first lecture?

    – what activity was scheduled from 11:00 to 12:00?

    – what activity took place from 1:00 to 3:00 PM?

32. What are the advantages of "repetitions" with a tutor?

33. Why did medieval universities require note-taking and the copying of books?

34. Of which character in Chaucer's *Canterbury Tales* was it said, "And gladly would he learn and gladly teach"?

35. Who was the patron saint of wandering scholars? What were the subjects of Goliardic verse?

36. Which century was the "Golden Age of the University of Paris"? Who was the most famous teacher of that century in Paris?

37. Why did Saint Francis of Assisi drop out of society and begin to lead a life of self denial?

38. Unlike monasteries of the early middle ages (established in the countryside "far from the madding crowd"), where were the centers of the Franciscans established?

39. What was the most important work of Thomas Aquinas (d. 1274)?

40. What was the answer of Aquinas to the problem of truth via reason vs. truth via divine revelation?

41. From what civilization did Europeans recover the lost works of Aristotle?

42. According to Avicenna (d. 1036) and Averroes of Cordova (d. 1198), was Aristotle's philosophy compatible with the faith of Islam?

43. According to Maimonides' *Guide for the Perplexed,* 1190 (written in Arabic), was the thought of Aristotle compatible with Hebrew scriptures?

44. What was the greatest work of fiction of the late middle ages (it has been considered the literary equivalent of Chartres Cathedral)?

45. In Botticelli's *Dante* (figure 10.16), why is Dante wearing a laurel wreath? Why do we call our leading poet a "poet laureate"?

46. Who was Dante's guide for the first two parts of his journey? For the third and last part?

47. What is the "happy ending" of Dante's *Divine Comedy*?

48. What was the importance of urbanization on the importance of monasteries as cultural centers?

49. What new social class evolved in the new cities of the High Middle Ages?

Thought Questions:

A. An important part of a student's day at the medieval University of Paris was taking part in "disputations" after the morning lectures. Why do you think students today do not take participate in disputations (discussions) after sitting in class lectures? Why would disputations add to a student's understanding of the subject?

B. Medieval universities had a required curriculum. Do you think colleges today should have required courses for a student's first two years? Why?

C. Are "distribution requirements" (the selection of courses from a list in specified academic areas) an acceptable alternative, or should there be some specific courses required for graduation? If you believe there should be specific courses, what should those courses be?

D. In the High Middle Ages, students from all over Europe chose to study at the University of Paris? Today why are students attracted to a specific university?

E. Which do you think the values of our culture emphasize most today, spirituality or materialism? Why?

Do not consider it proof just because it is written in books, for a liar who will deceive with his tongue will not hesitate to do the same with his pen.

– Maimonides (1135 – 1204)

Define or Identify:

Twelfth-century Renaissance (1100s)
Abbot Suger
- Gothic Architecture (Characteristics)
- Pointed Arch (vs. Round)
- Luminosity / Stained Glass
- Flying Buttress

Monastic Schools / Cathedral Schools
Universitas / Guild
University of Paris
Scholasticism

St. Francis of Assisi
- [Franciscans]

Significant Works To Recognize and Remember

Abbey Church of Saint Denis
Notre Dame Cathedral, Paris
Chartres Cathedral: "Notre Dame de Belle Verriere"
Sainte Chapelle, Paris

Peter Abelard, *Sic et Non* (*Yes and No*), 1121
Thomas Aquinas, *Summa Theologica* (Faith + Reason), c. 1267 – 1273
Dante, *Divine Comedy* (Hell, Purgatory, Heaven), c. 1303 – 1321
Chaucer, *Canterbury Tales*, c. 1385 – 1400
Maimonides, *Guide for the Perplexed,* 1190

CHAPTER 10 - REVIEW

Begin by writing the title of the chapter you've just studied. Next, without looking at the text or your study guide, use your memory to recall and to list the major sections or topics covered in the chapter. Finally, check your knowledge by taking the short "Self Quiz" below.

A) CHAPTER TITLE:

B) MAJOR SECTIONS OR TOPICS:

C) SELF QUIZ # 10 – IDENTIFY THE:

01. ______________ City which was the intellectual and cultural center of western Europe from 1150 to 1300.

02. ______________ Abbey church rebuilt and transformed into a new style of architecture by the Abbot Suger.

03. ______________ Most important style of architecture during the High Middle Ages (pointed arches/rib vaults).

04. ______________ Medieval cathedral (SW of Paris) famous for its 173 stained glass windows.

05. ______________ Most famous university in northern medieval Europe.

06. ______________ Most important scholar of the University of Paris in the early 1100s; author of *Sic et Non*.

07. ______________ Most important scholar of the University of Paris in the 1200s; author of *Summa Theologica*.

08. ______________ Country from which Europeans recovered the lost works of Aristotle.

09. ______________ Chaucer's book including a description of the medieval student, "Gladly would he learn and gladly teach."

10. ______________ Literary masterpiece by Dante describing a symbolic journey through hell, purgatory, and heaven.

10. WEB QUESTS - THE HIGH MIDDLE AGES

GEOFFREY CHAUCER (1342-1400) – THE CANTERBURY TALES
http://www.librarius.com/cantales.htm

– Read the General Prologue by click on "General Prologue" in the left frame.

– Read (on the right frame) lines 1–27 and 287–310. (Click on the underlined archaic words and see an instant definition in the lower right frame.)

01. In what month does the Tale begin? (Line 1)

02. From where in "Engaland" do the pilgrims come? (Line 15)

03. Why are they traveling to Canterbury? (Lines 16-18)

04. Who is described in line 287? Where was he educated?

05. What would he like to have at the head of his bed? (Line 295-298)

06. On what two things did he spend all his income? (Line 302)

07. What two things would he "gladly" do? (Line 310)

THOMAS BECKET
http://www.digiserve.com/peter/becket.htm

08. To what position in the English government was Becket appointed in 1154 by King Henry II?

09. What position in the Church did Becket achieve in 1162?

10. According to King Henry II, in which courts should members of the clergy be tried? According to Becket?

11. What were the words allegedly uttered about Becket by King Henry II?

12. What happened in Canterbury Cathedral on December 29, 1170?

13. In 1173, what action was taken by the Pope regarding Becket?

14. What did King Henry II do in penance?

DANTE ALIGHIERI – THE DIVINE COMEDY
http://www.italianstudies.org/comedy/Inferno1.htm
[CLICK on the above URL; then in the left margin of the page that appears, CLICK on "VOLUME 1: Inferno"]

15. How far through his mortal life was Dante when he wakened to find himself in a dark wood? (See Canto 1, Line 1)

16. What person appears to guide Dante through the Inferno and Purgatory ? (Read Canto 1, Lines 61 –87)

[CLICK on the number "3" in the left margin to go to Canto 3.]

17. What is the subject or setting of Canto/Canticle 3?

18. What are the last seven words found on the inscription of the Gate of Hell? (Canto 3, Lines 9–12)

19. Why are the group of souls seen by Dante in the vestibule to Hell ("rejected by God and not accepted by the powers of Hell) doomed to "nowhere"? (Canto 3, Lines 31–42)

11. THE FOURTEENTH CENTURY: A TIME OF TRANSITION

Study Questions:

CALAMITY, DECAY, AND VIOLENCE

01. What is the meaning of the term "Renaissance"?

02. What dramatic event in 1348 greatly reduced the population of Europe?

03. Why did the young people in Boccaccio's *Decameron* leave Florence to live in the country for ten days?

04. Why has the *Decameron* often been called the "Human Comedy" (in contrast to Dante's "*Divine" Comedy*)?

05. Where was the residence of the Papacy from 1309 to 1367? What name was given to this period of the papacy?

06. After the return of the papacy to Rome, what name was given to the split (1378-1417) in the Roman Catholic Church?

07. What was the basic question asked by the priest John Ball during the Peasants Revolt of 1381? How did his reference to Adam and Eve strengthen his argument? Where did the Peasants Revolt of 1381 take place?

08. To whom did the leaders of the towns of Europe turn for help against the feudal aristocracy?

09. What name was given to the Christian holy wars intended to capture Jerusalem for the West? What was the influence of these wars on the Byzantine Empire?

10. In 1299, what new dynasty was founded (it lasted until 1919) east of the Byzantine Empire?

11. What influence did the fall of Constantinople to the Turks in 1453 have on the Italian Renaissance? Why?

12. Which two European countries were the main combatants in the Hundred Years' War? What was the political question leading to the Hundred Years War?

13. What important weapon used at the Battle of Crecy (1346) contributed to the decline of knights in shining armor and an increase in the power of the infantry?

LITERATURE

14. Who was the most important Tuscan writer (1304 – 1374) of the 1300s, and why was he important? (Where is Tuscany?)

15. Who was crowned poet laureate of Rome in 1348 (the first artist so honored since ancient Rome)? What did his "crown" look like?

16. Who was the primary subject of the 300 sonnets and 49 canzoni (songs) in Petrarch's *Canzoniere* (*Songbook*)?

17. Who was the greatest English writer of the 1300s?

18. What is the narrative framework of Chaucer's *Canterbury Tales*?

19. Who are some of the characters introduced in the "General Prologue" to the *Canterbury Tales*?

20. Which character in the *Canterbury Tales* argues against misogyny and also sees sexual relations as a good given by God? (What is misogyny?)

21. Of which character in Chaucer's *Canterbury Tales* was it said, "And gladly would he learn and gladly teach"?

22. Who was one of the first women in medieval Europe to make a living as a professional writer? What was her most important book (1404)?

23. What was the theme of *The Book of the City of Ladies* (1404)? What method does the author use in the book to demonstrate the virtues of women?

ART IN ITALY

24. What book, published in 1550, was the earliest account of the rebirth of Italian art in the Renaissance? Who was its author?

25. Who was the first of the great Florentine painters discussed in Vasari's *Lives of the Artists* (1550)?

26. What was the preeminent characteristic of Giotto's art that allowed Vasari to credit him for "setting painting once again on the right path"?

27. Which cycle of frescoes constitutes Giotto's greatest claim to fame? In what city (and chapel) are they found?

28. What was the subject of Giotto's *Lamentation* (c. 1305)?

29. In Giotto's *Saint Francis Renouncing his Worldly Goods* (figure 11.11), how does the bishop react to Francis' nakedness? What action of the bishop symbolizes Francis' entry into the church?

30. What name is given to the art style of the 1300s that blended together Italian and Northern elements?

ART IN NORTHERN EUROPE

31. What is the subject of the *Wilton Diptych* (c. 1377)?

32. What city was one of the first great centers of the International Style? What Duke presided over its court?

33. Who was commissioned by the Duke of Burgundy to provide sculpture (*The Well of Moses*, 1406) for the Chartreuse monastery near Dijon?

34. What were the subjects of the twelve illuminated pages in *the Trés Riches Heures du Duc de Berry* (1416)? Who were the artists?

LATE GOTHIC ARCHITECTURE

35. How does Late Gothic architecture compare with Northern Gothic architecture, specifically

    – flying buttresses?

    – widespread use of glass windows in the walls?

36. What is the Italian word for cathedral? Why is this an appropriate name for the cathedral of Florence?

37. What architect was responsible for the magnificent dome of Florence Cathedral?

38. What name is given to the style of late Gothic architecture in England? Why?

<u>Thought</u> <u>Questions</u>:

A. Petrarch spent much of his life searching for ancient manuscripts. What three old books can you think of that would still be of value today? Have you read and did you learn anything from the three books?

B. Giotto is credited with the rediscovery of realistic painting. What makes a painting look realistic (or if you wish, why do so many medieval paintings, and some modern art not look realistic)?

Just as women's bodies are softer than men's, so their understanding is sharper.
– Christine de Pisan (1365 – 1428?)

Define or Identify:

Black Plague
Great Schism
Hundred Years' War
Renaissance
Illuminated Manuscripts (Review)
Ars Nova

Significant Works To Recognize and Remember

Cimabue, *Crucifixion*, c. 1240 – 1302; *Madonna Enthroned,* c. 1270 – 1285
Giotto, Arena Chapel frescoes, Padua
Pieta / Lamentation, 1306
Limbourg Brothers, *Trés Riches Heures du Duc de Berry*, 1416

Petrarch, "poet laureate", sonnets to Laura
Boccaccio, *Decameron*, 1352
Chaucer, *Canterbury Tales*, c. 1385 – 1400
Christine de Pisan, *Book of the City of Ladies*, 1404
Vasari, *Lives of the Artists*, 1550

Other Important Works (Not in the textbook)

The Lady and the Unicorn Tapestries, late 1400s
The Hunting of the Unicorn Tapestries, c. 1500

CHAPTER 11 - REVIEW

Begin by writing the title of the chapter you've just studied. Next, without looking at the text or your study guide, use your memory to recall and to list the major sections or topics covered in the chapter. Finally, check your knowledge by taking the short "Self Quiz" below.

A) CHAPTER TITLE:

B) MAJOR SECTIONS OR TOPICS:

C) SELF QUIZ # 11 – IDENTIFY THE:

01. ______________ Widespread cause of the great reduction of European population in 1348.

02. ______________ Name given to the great split in the Roman Catholic Church from 1378 to 1417.

03. ______________ War lasting more than a century (1337– 1453) between England and France.

04. ______________ Italian collector of ancient manuscripts and author of 300 sonnets to Laura; crowned poet laureate in 1348.

05. ______________ Boccaccio's book of 1352 in which ten young people tell a story a day for ten days while in the countryside.

06. ______________ Author of *The Canterbury Tales* and the greatest English writer of the 1300s.

07. ______________ Author of *The Book of the City of Ladies* (a defense of the virtues of women) and one of Europe's first women to make a living from writing books.

08. ______________ Italian painter known for "breaking with the past" and achieving a more realistic art in his Arena Chapel frescoes of the lives of the Virgin and Christ.

09. ______________ Brothers responsible for the illuminated pages in the *Trés Riches Heures du Duc de Berry* (1416).

10. ______________ Term meaning "new birth" of culture characteristic of fifteenth-century Europe.

11. WEB QUESTS - THE FOURTEENTH CENTURY

LES TRÈS RICHES HEURES DU DUC DE BERRY
http://www.christusrex.org/www2/berry/berry1.html
Examine the Very Rich Book of Hours of the Duke of Burgundy *for the months indicated and answer the questions below.*

January

01. Who is seated at the center of the table (dressed in blue, with a gold chain around his neck)?

02. What is the subject of the tapestry hanging on the wall?

February

03. What is the young man doing in the upper right? Why?

04. Why is the mistress of the household considered more modest than the two peasants?

05. What is hanging on the rods on the wall behind her?

April

06. What is the man in the red hat doing?

07. What is the reaction of the woman receiving his attention?

08. Who are the two people watching with approval?

June

09. What building is shown in the upper right-hand corner?

October

10. What building dominates this scene?

11. What was the function of this building? [This building was demolished in order to create a new modern palace for the King. But major portions of the original building were unearthed in 1983 and can be seen again today.]

THE LION AND THE UNICORN TAPESTRIES / *LA DAME À LA LICORNE*
http://www.musee-moyenage.fr/ang/homes/home_id20393_u1l2.htm
This is the home page of the Cluny Museum – France's National Museum of the Middle Ages. Next, click on the small icon of a unicorn, then click on "Explore the Collection."

12. What is the subject of the first five tapestries?

- Tapestry 1:
- Tapestry 2:
- Tapestry 3:
- Tapestry 4:
- Tapestry 5:

13. What is the subject of the sixth tapestry?

Click on each of the images for a larger image and then scroll to the bottom of each page for more information about each tapestry. You can also click on each of the three small icons in the upper right hand corner for close-ups of details.

14. In Tapestry 1, what is the lady selecting from the dish being offered to her by her servant?

15. In Tapestry 2, what image is reflected in the mirror held by the lady?

16. In Tapestry 3, what is the lady touching with her left hand?

17. In Tapestry 4, what is the lady making with her hands? What has the monkey taken from the basket and what is he doing with it? [*Click on the second and third small icons for close-ups.*]

18. In Tapestry 5, what instrument is being played by the lady?

19. In Tapestry 6, what is the translation of the inscription woven at the top of the tent (*A mon seul désire*)?

20. Is the lady placing her necklace in the casket (after taking it from her neck) or is she picking out a necklace?

21. What do you think is the meaning of Tapestry #6 if she is renouncing the jewelry?

22. What was the inspiration for Tracy Chevalier to write her book, *The Lady and the Unicorn* (2003)?
http://www.tchevalier.com/unicorn/inspiration/index.html

END OF SECTION REVIEW OF THE MIDDLE AGES

Match the descriptions with the correct answers:

_____	01.	Aachen	A.	Belief in only one God
_____	02.	Abbot Suger	B.	"Good News" of Matthew, Mark, etc.
_____	03.	Abelard	C.	Early symbol of Christianity
_____	04.	Alhambra	D.	Roman building used for churches
_____	05.	Allah	E.	Long, central space of a church
_____	06.	Aquinas	F.	Open courtyard in home or church
_____	07.	Atrium	G.	Emperor issuing edict of toleration
_____	08.	Baghdad	H.	Capital city of Eastern Roman Empire
_____	09.	Basilica	I.	Important church of Constantinople
_____	10.	Benedict	J.	Other name for Eastern Roman Empire
_____	11.	Boethius	K.	Manuscript book or volume
_____	12.	Byzantine Empire	L.	Earliest New Testament in Greek
_____	13.	Charlemagne	M.	Augustine's linear view of history
_____	14.	Chaucer	N.	Author of *Consolation of Philosophy*
_____	15.	*Chi-Rho* sign	O.	Art consisting of small stones
_____	16.	*City of God*	P.	Painting on fresh plaster
_____	17.	Codex	Q.	Image
_____	18.	*Codex Sinaiticus*	R.	Image-breaker
_____	19.	Constantine	S.	Messenger and prophet of Islam
_____	20.	Constantinople	T.	Most beautiful Mughal building
_____	21.	*Divine Comedy*	U.	Muslim building used for worship
_____	22.	*Everyman*	V.	Muslim name for God
_____	23.	Fresco	W.	City of "House of Wisdom," Abbasid Dynasty
_____	24.	Giotto	X.	Muslim palace in Granada, Spain
_____	25.	Gospel	Y.	Crowned emperor in AD 800
_____	26.	Gothic	Z.	Capital city of Charlemagne
_____	27.	Hagia Sophia	AA.	Writing developed by Carolingians
_____	28.	Icon	BB.	Grammar, Rhetoric, Logic
_____	29.	Iconoclast	CC.	Author of important monastic Rule
_____	30.	Limbourg Brothers	DD.	Beginnings of medieval drama
_____	31.	*Memento Mori*	EE.	Crusade against Muslim Spain
_____	32.	Minuscule	FF.	Oldest *chanson de geste*
_____	33.	Mohammed	GG.	Medieval morality play
_____	34.	Monotheism	HH.	Style of architecture, 1000-1150
_____	35.	Mosaics	II.	Style of architecture after 1150
_____	36.	Mosque	JJ.	Characteristic of Gothic architecture
_____	37.	Nave	KK.	"Father of Gothic architecture"
_____	38.	Notre Dame	LL.	First Gothic church
_____	39.	Paris	MM.	"Our Lady" [Mary]
_____	40.	Petrarch	NN.	First university in Northern Europe
_____	41.	Pointed Arch	OO.	Important teacher at Univ. of Paris
_____	42.	*Quem Queritas*	PP.	Author of the *Summa Theologica*
_____	43.	*Reconquista*	QQ.	"Gladly ... learn and gladly teach"
_____	44.	Renaissance	RR.	Collector of old Greek manuscripts
_____	45.	Romanesque	SS.	He rediscovering "real" painting
_____	46.	St. Denis	TT.	A journey through Hell to Heaven
_____	47.	Song of Roland	UU.	"Keep death before your eyes"
_____	48.	Taj Mahal	VV.	"Rebirth"
_____	49.	*Trivium*	WW.	Painters of the *Trés Riches Heures*
_____	50.	1453	XX.	Year Constantinople fell to the Turks

REVIEW II - B – GEOGRAPHY AND ART: THE MIDDLE AGES

YOUR ASSIGNMENT:

A) Use the maps in your textbook to identify the locations marked on the map below.

B) Match from the below list the work of art or architecture associated with the place you've identified:

A)	Location on map:	B)	Location of of work of art:
1. _____	ROME	_____	Abbey church of St. Denis
2. _____	RAVENNA	_____	Arnolfini Marriage
3. _____	CONSTANTINOPLE	_____	Charlemagne's Chapel
4. _____	AACHEN	_____	Hagia Sophia
5. _____	ST. DENIS	_____	Mosaics, Church of San Vitale
6. _____	PARIS	_____	Old St. Peter's Basilica
7. _____	CHARTRES	_____	Notre Dame de Belle Verrière
8. _____	BRUGES	_____	La Sainte Chapelle

12. *THE EARLY RENAISSANCE*

Study Questions:

THE EARLY RENAISSANCE

01. Which city was the most important center of the early Italian Renaissance?

02. How did success in the wool trade and in banking contribute to the support of artistic genius in Florence?

03. In Massacio's *The Holy Trinity* (1428), how is the Holy Spirit represented? (Can you see it between the faces of God and Jesus?) [Note also the lower section of the fresco, beneath the kneeling donors, which shows a skeleton with the inscription in Italian, "I was once that which you are; and that which I am you will become."]

04. In Masaccio's *The Tribute Money* (c. 1425),

– what three events are shown?

– how realistic is it to show these three events simultaneously?

– how has Masaccio painted the building on the right to help create a sense of depth in what is actually a flat fresco painted on the wall?

05. Who were the two most famous competitors in the 1401 competition for the decoration of the doors of the Florence Baptistery? Who won? Why?

06. For how many years did Lorenzo Ghiberti work on the North Doors of the Baptistery? on the East Doors? What name did Michelangelo give to Ghiberti's East Doors?

07. To which city did Brunelleschi go after losing the sculpture competition of 1401? Who was his companion? What was one result of the trip?

08. What was Brunelleschi's contribution to Florence Cathedral?

09. How did Brunelleschi's achievement later influence Michelangelo's design for Saint Peter's in the Vatican?

10. Who was the founder of the Renaissance style of architecture (the Foundling Hospital, Florence, 1419-26 and the Pazzi Chapel, Florence, 1430 – 1433)?

11. Which powerful and wealthy family ruled Florence from 1434 to 1492? What was the primary source of their wealth?

12. What was the subject of the famous Flemish painting in 1434 by Jan Van Eyck (figure 12.12)?

    – What materials were used in its creation?

    – Who is shown reflected in the mirror image on the wall?

    – What is the translation of the Latin words on the wall?

    – What is the symbolism

        – of the dog?

        – the single light in the candelabra?

        – the bride's apparent physical condition?

        – the shoes?

        – the whisk broom by the bed?

13. Who was the greatest Florentine sculptor of the first half of the 1400s? What family was his patron?

14. What was the subject of Donatello's most famous near-life size sculpture (and the first free-standing stature of a nude figure Roman antiquity)?

15. What stage in the fight against Goliath is shown in

    – Donatello's *David*? (figure 12.14)

    – Michelangelo's *David*? (figure 12.28)

    – Bernini's *David*? (figure 15.9)

16. Do you think Donatello's *David* (c. 1430 – 1432) emphasizes physical beauty or religious truth?

17. What thoughts did Donatello intend to provoke by his portrayal of *Saint Mary Magdalen* (1455) as an old woman ravaged by time?

THE ITALIAN RENAISSANCE: FROM LORENZO THE MAGNIFICENT

18. Who ruled Florence during the second half of the 1400s (the Laurentian Era)?

19. Why does *The Song of Bacchus* (1490) by Lorenzo de Medici advocate "let him be who chases joy"?

20. What are the two most famous paintings of Sandro Botticelli:

    – c. 1478: – 1480:

21. In Botticelli's *La Primavera*, what does the central female figure represent? Who hovers overhead? Who is the figure in the flowered dress?

22. How was Botticelli's *The Birth of Venus* influenced by Platonic idealism? By the Christian view of the Virgin Mary?

23. Which face in *La Primavera* is also the face of Venus in *The Birth of Venus*?

24. Which artist is considered the genius of the Italian Renaissance?

25. In Leonardo's *The Last Supper* (1495 – 1498), what precise moment has he chosen to depict?

26. What was the subject of Michelangelo's *Pietà* (1498)? How does it compare in composition and intensity with Giotto's *Lamentation over the Dead Christ*, 1305 (Fig 11.10)?

27. In Michelangelo's *David* (1501 – 1504),

    – what is David looking at?

    – what is he holding in his left hand?

    – what expression do you see on his face?

    – does his right hand seem in scale with the rest of his body?

    – is he "nude" or "naked"? What's the difference?

28. Why was Michelangelo's David placed outside the Palazzo Vecchio of Florence?

29. Which Dominican monk preached against Florentine art and culture? What were his criticisms?

30. According to Jacob Burckhardt's *The Civilisation of the Renaissance in Italy* (1860), how did the values and beliefs of the Renaissance differ from those of the Middle Ages?

31. What two earlier "renaissances" were there in the 800s and 1100s?

32. What were seen as the advantages of humanist education and learning?

33. What was the theme of Pico della Mirandola's *Oration on the Dignity of Man* (1486)?

34. After 1455, what "communications revolution" helped spread humanist learning of the Renaissance?

35. What German in 1455 invented printing with movable type?

36. What two styles of humanist learning are exemplified by the writing of Machiavelli and Erasmus?

37. Which book of Machiavelli is often considered the first purely secular study of political theory? According to Machiavelli, what was the role of morality in the exercise of power? According to Machiavelli, what justification was there for a prince to use cruelty or hypocrisy?

38. In the 1500s, who was the most important Christian humanist in Europe?

39. In Dürer's print, *Erasmus of Rotterdam* (figure 12.29),

    – What is Erasmus shown doing?

    – What is the meaning of the Latin words in the background (*IMAGO.ERASMI.ROTERODAMI.AB.ALBERTO.DVRERO. ADVIVAM.EFFIGIEM.DELINIATA*)?

    – What is the meaning of the monogram beneath the date?

40. What was the response of Erasmus to the possible conflict between classical learning and Christian living?

41. Why did Erasmus study and compare existing Greek manuscripts to prepare his *Greek New Testament* (1516)?

42. Which was the most famous book written by Erasmus? What were some of the targets of Erasmus' satire?

Thought Questions:

A. What did Burckhardt mean when he wrote that the great achievement of the Renaissance was "the discovery of the world and the discovery of man"?

B. Can (and should) humanity be considered a "great miracle"?

C. Should the *New Testament* be subjected to scholarly textual analysis?

Define or Identify:

Renaissance
Florence (the early Renaissance in Italy)
Humanism
    Christian Humanism
    Secular Humanism
Medici family
Savonarola

Significant Works To Recognize and Remember

Ghiberti
    Sacrifice of Isaac, 1401– 1402
    The Gates of Paradise, c. 1425 – 1453
Brunelleschi
    Florence Cathedral Dome, 1417 – 1436
    Foundling Hospital, Florence, 1419 – 1426
    Pazzi Chapel, Florence, 1430 – 1437
Masaccio
    The Tribute Money, c. 1425
    The Holy Trinity, 1428
Jan Van Eyck, *Giovanni Arnolfini and His Bride (Arnolfini Portrait),* 1434
Fra Angelico, *Annunciation*, 1450
Donatello, *David*, 1432
Botticelli
    La Primavera (Springtime), 1478
    The Birth of Venus, 1480
Leonardo da Vinci
    Last Supper, 1498
    Mona Lisa / La Gioconda, 1505
Michelangelo
    Pietà, 1499
    David, 1501 – 1504
    [See also other works in Chapter 13]

Gutenberg *Bible*, 1455
Pico della Mirandola, *Oration on the Dignity of Man*, 1486
Machiavelli, *The Prince*, 1513
Erasmus
    In Praise of Folly, 1509
    Greek New Testament, 1516

CHAPTER 12 - REVIEW

Begin by writing the title of the chapter you've just studied. Next, without looking at the text or your study guide, use your memory to recall and to list the major sections or topics covered in the chapter. Finally, check your knowledge by taking the short "Self Quiz" below.

A) CHAPTER TITLE:

B) MAJOR SECTIONS OR TOPICS:

C) SELF QUIZ # 12 – IDENTIFY THE:

01. ________________ First important city of the Italian Renaissance.

02. ________________ Artist of the North and East Doors ("The Gates of Paradise") of the Baptistery of Florence Cathedral.

03. ________________ Brunelleschi's contribution to Florence Cathedral.

04. ________________ Most important family and patrons of Florence.

05. ________________ Sculptor of *David* (1432), the first freestanding nude figure since Roman antiquity.

06. ________________ Painter in oil of *Giovanni Arnolfini and His Bride* (1434).

07. ________________ Artist of *La Primavera (Springtime)* and *The Birth of Venus.*

08. ________________ Painter of the *Last Supper* and the *Mona Lisa*; a "renaissance man" interested in all things.

09. ________________ Values ("ism") advocated by Pico della Mirandola (*Oration On the Dignity of Man*).

10. ________________ Author of *The Prince.*

11. ________________ Most important Christian Humanist of the early 1500s (*Greek New Testament, The Praise of Folly*).

12. ________________ Dominican preacher and reformer strongly opposed to the vanities of Florence, especially its art and culture.

12. WEB QUESTS - THE EARLY RENAISSANCE

THE ADORATION OF THE MAGI
http://www.nga.gov/collection/adoration.htm
This three-minute Real Audio / Video from the National Gallery (Washington, D.C.) will load automatically when you go to the above URL.

01. How many days after the birth of Christ did the Three Kings appear bearing gifts?

02. What is meant by the "Epiphany"? On what day is it celebrated? Why?

03. Why is the king in the pale rose robe leaning forward and kneeling?

04. What medieval symbol suggests immortality?

05. What Renaissance symbol represents the idea of the new Christian religion rising from the ruins of paganism?

LEONARDO DA VINCI
- LEONARDO'S PERSPECTIVE
http://www.mos.org/sln/Leonardo/LeonardosPerspective.html

"The most praiseworthy form of painting is the one that most resemble what it imitates." – Leonardo

06. Do you agree with Leonardo's statement? Why?

07. What two or three other definitions of "praiseworthy" painting might there be?

- LEONARDO'S WINDOW
http://www.mos.org/sln/Leonardo/LeonardosWindow.html

08. What does it mean to you to see, as Leonardo did, a painting as an "open window?

09. What way could a painting be seen other than as a "window".

- EXPLORING LINEAR PERSPECTIVE
http://www.mos.org/sln/Leonardo/ExploringLinearPerspective.html

10. What is the goal of "linear perspective"? (The creation on a flat surface the _________ of ________ and _______.)

11. What three elements of linear perspective are demonstrated in Leonardo's painting of the *Annunciation*?
[See the visual demonstration in the middle of the web page.]

- THE LAST SUPPER – LOCATION, TECHNIQUE, CONTENT AND FORM
http://ccat.sas.upenn.edu/~lbianco/project/history.html

12. In what year did Leonardo begin painting *The Last Supper*? In what year did he finish it?

13. Why did Leonardo use a nail and string in painting *The Last Supper?*

14. What precise moment has Leonardo chosen to depict?

15. Why did Leonardo in his desire to show expressive characterization for each of the disciples not use a circular or round table as had been traditional?

16. What is striking about Leonardo's geometric composition of the Apostles?

17. What may be the symbolism of showing Christ in the form of a triangle?

18. Which figure is Judas?

THE MONA LISA
http://www.pbs.org/treasuresoftheworld/a_nav/mona_nav/main_monafrm.html

19. What happened to the *Mona Lisa* on August 21, 1911?

[For the end of the story, CLICK on "Mona's Return" at the bottom of the screen.]

20. Why did Vincenzo Leonard take the *Mona Lisa*?

21. What happened to the *Mona Lisa* on January 4th, 1914?

22. Thought Question: What do you think should be rightful place for the *Mona Lisa*?

WHY IS THE MONA LISA SMILING?
http://library.thinkquest.org/13681/data/link2.htm?tqskip1=1

23. According to Dr. Lillian Schwartz of Bell Laboratories, who posed for the famous portrait of the Mona Lisa?

24. How did she reach her conclusion?

13. *THE HIGH RENAISSANCE IN ITALY*

Study Questions:

ROME: THE HIGH RENAISSANCE

01. Which city is most associated with the High Renaissance in Italy?

02. Which Pope (from 1503 to 1513) is most associated with the beginning of the High Renaissance in Rome?

03. In Rome, who was the most important patron of Michelangelo and Raphael?

04. In Raphael's *School of Athens* (1510 – 1511),

– who are the two philosophers in the center?

– who is shown sprawled in front of the two philosophers?

– in the lower right corner of the fresco, who is shown looking out at the viewer?

– what does this painting, hanging in the Vatican, suggest about the views of Julius II toward humanist beliefs?

05. While Raphael was painting the *School of Athens*, who was working a few yards away from him in the Sistine Chapel?

06. Which Renaissance sculptor is associated with the belief that his role was to carve away the excess in a block of marble to reveal the figure within?

07. Who called Michelangelo to Rome in 1505? Why?

08 Where in the Sistine Chapel are the most famous frescoes of Michelangelo? What are the subjects of the three center panels?

09. What extra information did Michelangelo add to his signature on the ceiling of the Sistine Chapel?

10. In Michelangelo's *Creation of Adam*, why is the finger of God reaching out?

11. What is the subject of the huge fresco painted (1534 – 1541) by Michelangelo on the wall behind the main altar of the Sistine Chapel? Whose face was used for Saint Bartholomew (see figure 13.10)?

12. Which Pope commissioned in 1506 the rebuilding of St. Peter's Basilica? What did Michelangelo add to Bramante's original design?

13. WEB QUESTS - THE HIGH RENAISSANCE IN ITALY

MICHELANGELO
http://www.michelangelo.com/buon/bio-index2.html

EARLY LIFE: 1475 – 1504

01. What was Michelangelo's father's reaction when his son told him he wanted to be an artist? What was the reason for the father's reaction?

02. What is the facial expression of Mary in Michelangelo's *Pietà*?

03. What is the meaning of the inscription
MICHEL ANGELUS BONAROTUS FLORENT FACIBAT
on the sash running across Mary's breast?

04. How many works did Michelangelo sign afterwards? Why?

05. What statue is considered to be the high point of Michelangelo's early style in Florence?

06. How would you describe the facial expression on Michelangelo's *David*?

MID YEARS: 1505 – 1535

07. What was Michelangelo's most important work between 1508 and 1512?

08. What scene is at the center of the Sistine Chapel ceiling?

FINAL DAYS: 1536 – 1564

09. What was the subject of Michelangelo's last major fresco in the Sistine Chapel?

10. How was this work of Michelangelo amended by the Council of Trent?

11. What is striking about Michelangelo's image in *The Last Judgement*?
(His face is the one in the center and to the center.)

12. What was Michelangelo's crowning achievement as an architect?

THE SISTINE CHAPEL - "HISTORY PANELS"
http://www.science.wayne.edu/~mcogan/Humanities/Sistine/Ceiling/index.html
CLICK on each of the "History Panel" links below and then answer the questions.

13. History Panel 1

a) What is the subject of this panel?

b) What is between the light and the dark areas of this panel?

14. History Panel 2

    a) What is being created at the left side of the panel?

    b) On the right side of the panel, what is next to
    God's right hand? God's left hand?

    c) Click on "New Cleaned" to compare the unrestored and restored work.
    What has become clearest, the plants, the sun, or the moon?

15. History Panel 4

    a) What is God about to give to the almost fully formed Adam?

    b) Who appears to be under the left arm of God?

16. History Panel 5

    a) What is the subject of this panel?

    b) What do you think God might be saying to Eve?

17. History Panel 6

    a) What is the subject of this panel?

    b) What is unusual about the appearance of the snake? (Why can the snake be described as anthropomorphic?)

    c) What is the symbolic significance of the tree?

    d) Compare the restored and unrestored versions.
    Which do you prefer? Why?

BELLINI'S THE FEAST OF THE GODS (National Gallery of Art, Washington, D.C.)
http://www.nga.gov/collection/gallery/gg17/gg17-1141.0.html
Take the tour "The Feast of the Gods," to examine this famous painting by Bellini and Titian, and then answer the below questions:

18. Why did Priapus, the god of virility, demand an annual sacrifice of a donkey?

19. Identify the principal figures in the painting:

    a) a woodland god attended by his donkey:

    b) the infant god of wine crowned with grape leaves:

    c) the messenger of the gods carrying his caduceus or herald's staff:

d) the king of the gods accompanied by an eagle:

e) a satyr with a grape wreath who blows on his shepherd's pipes:

f) the god of the sea sitting beside his trident harpoon:

g) the goddess of cereal grains with a wreath of wheat:

h) god of the sun and the arts, crowned by laurel and holding a Renaissance stringed musical instrument:

20. After Bellini's death, in what ways did Titian alter the painting?

21. Thought Question: What is your about the right of the owner of the work of art to make changes to the work because it is his or her private property and no longer the property of the artist?

CAPPELLA SISTINA
http://www.christusrex.org/www1/sistine/0-Tour.html
For those with DSL or other broadband connections, check out the above site for the largest and clearest images of the Sistine Chapel, both the ceiling and the Last Judgment. These are very large images and will take time to load.

14. THE RENAISSANCE IN THE NORTH

Study Questions:

THE REFORMATION

01. Which country in southern Europe most influenced the Renaissance in northern Europe?

02. Which French king (1515 – 1547) exposed French culture to Italian influences by attracting to his court artists such as Leonardo da Vinci and Benvenuto Cellini?

03. Why was the Hapsburg emperor Charles V able to bring Italian influences to Germany as well as to Spain?

04. Which family ruled England (1585 –1603) during most of the Renaissance period? Who was the last ruler (1558 –1603) of this family?

05. With what dramatic event in 1517 did the Reformation begin?

06. Why was Luther critical of indulgences? How was the rebuilding of St. Peter's in Rome related to the practice of indulgences?

07. What were Luther's views on the

    – use of statues by the church?

    – right of clergy to marry?

    – number of sacraments?

08. Who was the leader of the Reformation in Geneva?

09. Which areas of Europe remained faithful to Roman Catholicism? Which were converted to Protestantism?

10. What new political force contributed to the success of the Protestant Reformation?

11. What views did humanists and reformers often share about the following:

    – monasticism?

    – intellectual preparation of the clergy?

    – the need for careful study of the Bible using the original Hebrew and Greek texts?

12. Who was responsible for the important translation of the Bible into German in 1521? into English in 1611?

13. What differences were there between humanists and religious reformers, specifically

    – the belief in human perfectibility through education?

    – the use of books other than the Bible as a source of religious truth?

14. What was the doctrine of "universal priesthood" ("the priesthood of all believers")? What influence did this belief have on the establishment of public education? Why?

15. According to Max Weber, what was the relationship between Calvinism and Capitalism?

16. What was the influence of the Protestant Reformation on literacy in Europe? Why did Luther want free education for all children in Germany?

17. What was the purpose of the *Index* of the Roman Catholic Church?

18. Did the culture of the Protestant Reformation emphasize words or pictures?

19. What was the influence of the Protestant Reformation on the sacred religious arts in northern Europe?

20. Why did Luther stress the importance of the vernacular hymn? (What does "vernacular" mean?) What was the most famous hymn written by Luther?

21. How was Calvin's church of St. Peter's in Geneva physically transformed from a Catholic cathedral to a reformed Protestant church?

22. What became the center of attention of the reformed church, the high altar or the pulpit? Why?

INTELLECTUAL DEVELOPMENTS

23. What word did Michel Montaigne use for his written short meditations?

24. Define the "generous nondogmatism" characteristic of the essays of Montaigne. What would be the opposite of "generous nondogmatism"? Why would anyone be dogmatic and not generous?

25. Why would the authority of Aristotle be an obstacle for scientists searching for the truth, especially those wishing to use the new scientific method advocated by Francis Bacon's *Novum Organum* (*New Instrument*) of 1620? [The "new instrument" was inductive reasoning, that is, proceeding from particular facts to

a general principle. Inductive reasoning emphasized conducting experiments, drawing conclusions, and testing the results with more experiments.]

26. In what respect did Copernicus' *On the Revolutions of Celestial Bodies* (1543) establish a breach between "common sense truth" and "scientific truth"?

27. Why did Copernicus' "heliocentric" view of the universe upset many people?

THE VISUAL ARTS IN NORTHERN EUROPE

28. Who were the three greatest German painters of the early 1500s?

29. Whose image is suggested by Dürer's *Self-Portrait* of 1500?

30. In Dürer's *Knight, Death, and the Devil* (1513), what is the reaction of the knight to the appearance of the Devil and Death? What is the meaning of the letters and numbers on the plaque in the lower-left hand corner?

31. What does the image of Christ in the *Isenheim Altarpiece* (1515) suggest about Grünewald's interest in the Renaissance conception of ideal beauty and the humanist interest in classical antiquity? in creating a painful, tortured image of Christ's crucifixion?

32. What subject of most western art (going back to the ancient Greeks), is missing from Altdorfer's *Danube Landscape near Regensburg* (c. 1525)? What does this suggest about the relative importance of nature for Altdorfer?

33. Who were the two greatest Netherlandish painters of the 1500s?

34. In Bosch's *Garden of Earthly Delights* (1510), what is the subject of the left wing of the triptych? of the center? of the right wing?

35. In what way are the paintings of Bruegel the Elder similar to those of Bosch? In what respect is Bruegel more of a humanist?

36. What is the general mood of Bruegel's *Peasant Wedding Feast* (1566 -- 1567)? Which figure do you think represents the bride? the bride's mother? the groom?

37. What mood is suggested by the colors in Bruegel's *Hunters in the Snow* (1565)? Have the hunters been successful?

FRANCE AND ENGLAND

38. What dynasty ruled the English throne from 1485 to 1603? Who was the last ruler of this dynasty (1588 – 1603)?

39. Which English king in 1534 separated the Church of England from the Roman Catholic Church?

40. What country was the subject of, and what spirit was expressed by these lines:

    This royal throne of kings, this sceptered isle, ...
    This happy breed of men, this little world, ...
    This blessed plot, this earth, this realm, this ....

41. Who was the best known painter to work for Henry VIII?

42. What was the name of the secular (non-religious) songs written in England by William Byrd to be performed at home by a small groups for their own entertainment?

43. What was the subject of Sir Thomas More's *Utopia* (1516)?

44. Which English dramatist was the subject of Ben Jonson's "He was not of an age, but for all time"?

45. What "two star-crossed lovers" were the subject in 1595 of Shakespeare's first great tragedy?

46. What is the name of the type of speech delivered by an actor alone on stage or unheard by others and used by Shakespeare to reveal the inner feelings of a character?

Thought Questions:

A. Are people influenced by what they read, or watch, or hear? Should censorship be a responsibility of the state? of the church? of parents?

B. Do you think books are as important for learning today or is the written word being replaced by the visual communication of television and film?

C. Do you think science should rely on experimentation and observation or on authority? Why?

Define or Identify:

Protestant Reformation
Luther, Wittenberg, 1517
Indulgences
"Universal Priesthood"
Calvin, Geneva
King Henry VIII, England
Queen Elizabeth I, England
King Philip II, Spain
Index
Copernicus, Heliocentric Theory
Linear Perspective
Triptych
Madrigals
Soliloquy

Significant Works To Recognize and Remember

Dürer, *Self-Portrait*, 1500*; Knight, Death and the Devil,* 1513
Cranach, *Martin Luther*, c. 1526
Grünewald, *Isenheim Altarpiece,* 1515
Bosch, *Garden of Earthly Delights* (triptych), c. 1505 – 1510
Bruegel, *Peasant Wedding Feast*, c. 1567; *Hunters in the Snow,* 1565
Luther, *Ninety-Five Theses*, 1517; German *Bible*
More, *Utopia*, 1516
Montaigne, *Essays*, 1590 – 1592 ["the journey, not the destination"]
Shakespeare, *Romeo and Juliet*, 1595; *Hamlet*, 1603

Other Important Works (Not in the textbook)

Jan & Hubert van Eyck, *Ghent Altarpiece*, c. 1432
Jan van Eyck, *Man in a Red Turban* (*Self Portrait*), 1433
Holbein, *The Ambassadors*, 1533
Bruegel, *Children's Games*, 1560; *Netherlandisch Proverbs*, 1560

What a piece of work is a man!
In form and moving how express and admirable!
In action how like an angel!
In apprehension how like a God!

– Shakespeare, *Hamlet* (Act II, Scene ii)

CHAPTER 14 - REVIEW

Begin by writing the title of the chapter you've just studied. Next, without looking at the text or your study guide, use your memory to recall and to list the major sections or topics covered in the chapter. Finally, check your knowledge by taking the short "Self Quiz" below.

A) CHAPTER TITLE:

B) MAJOR SECTIONS OR TOPICS:

C) SELF QUIZ # 14 – IDENTIFY THE:

01. ______________ German religious reformer questioning indulgences in his 95 Theses of 1517; he also translated the Bible into German.

02. ______________ Leader of the Protestant Reformation in Geneva.

03. ______________ German credited with the invention of printing with movable type.

04. ______________ List of books prohibited by the Roman Catholic Church.

05. ______________ Word used by Montaigne for his written, short meditations ("The journey, not the arrival, matters").

06. ______________ Greatest German artist (especially his woodcuts) of the early 1500s (*Knight, Death, and the Devil*, 1513).

07. ______________ Greatest Netherlandish artist of the early 1500s (*Garden of Earthly Delights*).

08. ______________ Greatest Netherlandish artist of the mid-1500s (*Peasant Wedding Feast*, 1567, *Hunters in the Snow*, 1565).

09. ______________ Type of speech delivered by an actor alone on stage or unheard by others and used by Shakespeare to reveal the inner feelings of a character.

10. ______________ A painting consisting of three panels.

14. WEB QUESTS - THE NORTHERN RENAISSANCE

PORTRAIT OF A MAN (1433)
http://www.nationalgallery.org.uk/cgi-bin/WebObjects.dll/CollectionPublisher.woa/wa/work?workNumber=NG222

01. What is the meaning of the inscriptions "ALS ICH KAN" and "MCCC . 33." on the frame?

02. Who may be the subject of this portrait?

HOLBEIN'S *THE AMBASSADORS* (1533)
http://gallery.euroweb.hu/html/h/holbein/hans_y/1535a/
The man on the left is the French ambassador to England, and the other man is his friend. They are depicted with their prize possessions on display. [Click on each image to see a much larger picture.]

03. Identify at least two objects on the shelves.

04. What object can be seen in the upper left hand corner of the painting?

05. What is the strange distorted object at the bottom and between the two men? **http://myweb.tiscali.co.uk/artofanamorphosis/skull.html**

06. Why do you think Holbein would place a distorted skull in his painting?

07. Review Question: What is a *memento mori?*

08. What personal possessions would you want included with your personal portrait? Why would you would like to have them included?

BOSCH
http://www.boschuniverse.org/
If necessary, CLICK on the Red, White, and Blue flag for the English version. Then CLICK on "His Works." Then, CLICK on "Tryptych" and look at the list of his works that will open on the right hand side of the page. Then CLICK on The Haywain.

09. Why is this called a "triptych"? *(CLICK on the word "Open" above the triptych, then CLICK on "Close", then CLICK on "Open" again.)*

10. What three scenes are shown in the open triptych? *(For information CLICK on the word "description" beneath the painting. For more information, CLICK on each panel to see an enlarged image, and then CLICK on "description" beneath the enlargements.)*

    a. Left: b. Center: c. Right:

11. What is the lesson of the central panel?

12. Who does the figure on the outside of the triptych represent and what is making his journey through life difficult? *(Be sure the triptych is closed. Then CLICK on the outside image (the man walking down the road) to get a larger Image. Then CLICK on the word "description" to the right of the larger image in order to read a description and explanation of the outer image of the altar piece.)*

BRUEGEL'S *CHILDREN'S GAMES* (1559-60)
http://www.artchive.com/artchive/ftptoc/bruegel_ext.html
Wait for the Artchive page to open, the click on "Image List," then click on "Children's Games".

13. Look carefully at the games played by children in Bruegel's time. Find three examples of games still played by children today. What are their names?

    a.

    b.

    c.

BRUEGEL'S NETHERLANDISCH PROVERBS (1560)
http://www.artchive.com/artchive/B/bruegel/proverbs.jpg.html
Discover how many old Dutch proverbs from Bruegel's "Netherlandisch Proverbs" are still used as English sayings today. Look carefully and locate the below proverbs, which can be seen in the bottom half of the painting.

a) It's like beating your head against a brick wall.

b) Covering someone with a cloak of deceit.

c) Casting roses (pearls) before swine.

d) You have to get pretty low to get through this world.

e) He's got the world in the palm (on the thumb) of his hand.

f) There's no sense crying over spilt milk.

15. THE BAROQUE WORLD

Study Questions:

THE BAROQUE WORLD IN ITALY, FRANCE, AND SPAIN

01. What was the response of the Roman Catholic Church to criticism of its beliefs in purgatory, transubstantiation, and celibacy for the clergy?
(What is meant by the doctrine of "transubstantiation"?)

02. What was the name of the military religious order founded by Ignatius Loyola? Why was it so successful?

03. What was the name of the predominant art style of the 1600s and early 1700s?

04. What was the attitude of the Roman Catholic Church to Baroque art and architecture? Why?

05. What are the characteristics of Baroque art?

06. Why did Caravaggio refuse to paint idealized versions of religious scenes?

07. Why did Caravaggio surround his figures with shadows instead of placing them in elaborate settings?

08. What is the name of the technique in painting involving the use of strong contrasts between light and dark?

09. How did Caravaggio use *chiaroscuro* to increase the dramatic impact of his *The Calling of Saint Matthew* (1598)?

10. Who has been called "the first woman in the history of the western world to make a significant contribution to the art of her time"? What was her most famous painting?

11. Who was the most important Italian sculptor of the Baroque Age?

12. How does the action of Bernini's *David* (1623) compare with that of Donatello's *David* (c. 1426 – 1432) and Michelangelo's *David* (1501 – 1504)?

13. What is happening in Bernini's *Ecstasy of St. Teresa*?

14. Who was the most important Baroque architect of Rome?
What was his most important contribution to the architecture of Rome?

15. Using the illustration of the basilica of St. Peter's in Rome (see figure 15.1), identify the piazza and the colonnade

16. Which French artist (1590 – 1652) was close in technique to Caravaggio? What technique of Caravaggio's was reflected in the candlelit scenes of this French artist?

17. What region of Greece was used to refer to an imaginary land of perfect peace and beauty? What is the theme of Poussin's *Et in Arcadia Ego*? Who is the "Ego" ("I") who is also in Arcadia?

18. Who was the subject of the most important portrait made by Hyacinthe Rigaud (1701)?

19. Which French king was called the "Sun King"? How did he use the Palace of Versailles to increase his power? Which is the most impressive room in the Palace of Versailles?

20. Which artistic style is reflected in the external decoration of the Palace of Versailles? In the scale of the structure (and its gardens)?

21. Who was the greatest painter in Spain in the 1500s? Which city is most associated with him? Why?

22. In El Greco's *Burial of Count Orgaz*, what is happening to the Count in the lower half of the painting? in the upper half? Is the mood of this painting one of repose or of emotion?

23. Who was the greatest Spanish painter (1599 – 1660) of the Baroque period?

24. In *Las Meninas / The Maids of Honor* (1651),

    – what two distinguished visitors can be seen reflected in the mirror?

    – at whom is the artist looking, the viewer, or the king and queen?

    – what is the significance of the red cross on the artist's breast (it was painted on after his death)?

BAROQUE ART IN NORTHERN EUROPE

25. Which two artists in northern Europe (both Flemish by birth) produced art for the aristocracy rather than for the middle class?

26. Who was the subject of many of Rubens' paintings during the last ten years of his life (1630 – 1640)? Why?

27. Who was the subject of the twenty-four enormous paintings created by Rubens between 1622 and 1625? How was he able to create so many paintings in a short period of time?

28. Who was Ruben's most famous assistant?

29. Why did Van Dyck paint his noble subjects the way they thought they looked rather than as they actually looked?

30. Why did Dutch painters have to depend on the tastes and demands of the open market rather than the patronage of the Roman Catholic Church or the Dutch Reformed Church?

31. Why were group portraits a common subject for Dutch painters such as Frans Hals (*Banquet of the Office of the Civic Guard of Saint George at Haarlem*)?

32. Which Dutch artist is best known for his <u>quiet</u> scenes of ordinary domestic life (a woman reading a letter, playing music, or making lace)?

33. How much emotion is expressed in Vermeer's *Woman Reading A Letter* (1662 – 1664)?

34. What was the subject of Rembrandt's *The Night Watch*? What are some of the ways Rembrandt made this an action picture instead of a conventional group portrait? What is inaccurate about the popular title of *The Night Watch*?

35. What technique of Caravaggio was also used by Rembrandt?

36. In what respect are Rembrandt's biblical paintings also secular and humanistic?

BAROQUE MUSIC

37. What was the most important new form of music to appear in the 1600s? In what city did it first appear?

38. What is the important difference between opera and other theatrical plays?

39. Who was the first great genius (1567 – 1643) in the history of opera?

40. What story from Greek mythology was the subject of Monteverdi's *Orfeo* (1607)?

41. What was added (by Jean Baptiste Lully and Jean Philippe Rameau) to opera performances at Versailles, the court of Louis XIV?

42. How do oratorios differ from opera (which are staged musical plays)? What was the source of the stories that were the subjects of oratorios?

43. In music, what is the term for a virtuoso composition from a keyboard instrument?

44. What is the difference between a sonata and a cantata?

45. What keyboard instrument is usually associated with the works of Domenico Scarlatti (1685 – 1757)?

46. What was Georg Friedrich Handel's (1685 – 1759) most important oratorio (1742)? His two most important orchestral works?

47. What three composers were born in 1685? Which one is generally considered to be the greatest musician of the Baroque period?

48. How did Bach's *Brandenburg Concertos* differ from the religious themes of his other works (such as the *Saint Matthew Passion*)?

PHILOSOPHY AND SCIENCE

49. What was the Ptolemaic view of the Universe? the Copernican? Which view was supported by the Church? Why?

50. How did Galileo want his theories to be tested, by the use of authorities (such as Aristotle) or by observation (as through a telescope)? Why?

51. Which French philosopher (1596 – 1650) is often called the "Father of Modern Philosophy"? What is the meaning of his phrase, *Cogito, ergo sum*?

52. Which English philosopher (1588 – 1679) is associated with the statement, "All that is real is material, and what is not material is not real"?

53. Why would Hobbes' "materialism" lead him to work on political problems rather than theological?

54. What political philosophy is advocated in Hobbes' *Leviathan* (1651)? Why?

55. According to Hobbes, what did individuals achieve by giving up their personal liberty to organize a government? What form of government would offer the greatest security?

56. According to Hobbes, which posed the greatest threat to security: other humans or the government?

57. What was John Locke's most influential work (1690) on ideas and learning? According to Locke, are ideas innate? If not, from where do they come?

LITERATURE IN THE SEVENTEENTH CENTURY

58. What three French dramatists benefited from the patronage of King Louis XIV?

59. Who was the creator of French Baroque comedy? What were the targets of his comedies?

60. Who were the two greatest French tragedians of the Baroque period?

61. What is the greatest novel in the Spanish language?

62. What would you think of a world that has little time for romance or honor? Can an individual add romance and honor to the world?

63. What work is often considered the greatest English literary achievement of the 1600s (the only great work of literature produced by a committee)?

64. What is generally considered to be the greatest epic poem in English of the 1600s?

65. How did Milton's *Paradise Lost* (1669) deal with the conflict between humanism and Christianity?

Thought Questions:

A. Should great events in biblical or secular history be shown using only images of idealized human beings?

B. Why are Rembrandt's self portraits considered great art?

C. It has been said that for those who think, life is a comedy, while for those who feel, life is a tragedy. Are you more inclined to see life as a comedy, or as a tragedy? Why?

D. Do you think the purpose of Cervantes' *Don Quixote* was to satirize a foolish dreamer, or a world in which dreamers look like fools?

E. Is it important to have dreams (sometimes impossible dreams)?

The actions of men are the best interpreters of their thoughts.
– John Locke (1632 – 1704)

Define or Identify:

Counter-Reformation / Catholic Reformation
(Italy, Spain, Austria)
Baroque
Chiaroscuro
Palace of Versailles (Hall of Mirrors)
King Louis XIV
Descartes, *Cogito, ergo sum*
Hobbes, "materialism"

Opera
Arias
Oratorio
Fugue

Significant Works To Recognize and Remember

Caravaggio, *Calling of St. Matthew*, 1598
Gentileschi, *Judith and Holofernes*, c. 1620
Bernini, *David*, 1624; St. Peter's Piazza; *Ecstasy of St. Teresa*, 1652
Poussin, *Et in Arcadia Ego*, 1639
Rigaud, *Portrait of Louis XIV*, 1701
El Greco, *Burial of Count Orgaz*, 1586
Velázquez, *Las Meninas* (*The Maids of Honor*), 1651
Rubens, *Journey of Marie de' Medici; Hélène Fourment*, 1637
Vermeer, *Woman Reading a Letter*, 1664
Rembrandt, *The Night Watch*, 1642; *Self-Portrait*, 1669

Monteverdi, *Orfeo* (opera), 1607
J. S. Bach, *Brandenburg Concertos*, 1721
Handel, *Messiah* (oratorio), 1742
Thomas Hobbes, *Leviathan* (Absolutism), 1651; Materialism
John Locke, *Essay Concerning Human Understanding*, 1690
(knowledge not innate, but from perception/senses)
Cervantes, *Don Quixote,* 1615
King James Bible, 1611
Milton, *Paradise Lost*, 1667

Other Important Works (Not in the textbook)

El Greco, *View of Toledo*, 1595-1600
Georges de la Tour, *Repentant Magdalen*, c. 1640 – 1645

CHAPTER 15 - REVIEW

Begin by writing the title of the chapter you've just studied. Next, without looking at the text or your study guide, use your memory to recall and to list the major sections or topics covered in the chapter. Finally, check your knowledge by taking the short "Self Quiz" below.

A) CHAPTER TITLE:

B) MAJOR SECTIONS OR TOPICS:

C) SELF QUIZ # 15 – IDENTIFY THE:

01. ________________ Most important art style of the 1600s.

02. ________________ Most important architect in Rome (St. Peter's Piazza) during this period.

03. ________________ Term used in painting meaning the use of strong contrasts between light and dark.

04. ________________ Artist who used this technique in his *Calling of St. Matthew, c. 1597– 1601.*

05. ________________ Dutch artist best known for quiet scenes of home life (*Woman Reading a Letter*).

06. ________________ Dutch artist remembered for his *Night Watch* and his many self portraits.

07. ________________ New form of music which consisted of a play in which the text was sung rather than spoken.

08. ________________ English philosopher associated with "materialism" and "absolutism"; author of *Leviathan*, 1651.

09. ________________ Palace used to increase the power of Louis XIV.

10. ________________ French philosopher and "Father of Modern Philosophy" ("*Cogito, Ergo Sum*").

11. ________________ Greatest Spanish Baroque artist (*Las Meninas / The Maids of Honor*, 1656)

12. ________________ Most important female Baroque painter in Rome, (*Judith and Holfernes*, 1620)

15. WEB QUESTS - THE BAROQUE WORLD

GEORGES DE LA TOUR
http://gallery.euroweb.hu/html/l/la_tour/georges/1/index.html

- **THE PENITENT MAGDALENE, c. 1638 – 1643**
  Scroll to the last two pictures on the page and click on them to see large images. The Penitent Magdalene *is the last image on the page; you can click on the "I" to the right for more "Information."*

01. What two signs of wealth are there on the table? On the floor?

02. What has she done with her jewelry?

03. What question do you think she is trying to answer?

- **THE MAGDALENE WITH THE SMOKING FLAME, c. 1640**

04. What two objects (in front of the books) reminds us of Christ's suffering?

05. Which of the two pictures do you prefer? Why?

06. Why is it appropriate to use the term *chiaroscuro* for these two works?

REMBRANDT, SELF PORTRAITS (Born 1606, died 1669)
http://www.mystudios.com/rembrandt/rembrandt-index.html
Click on Self Portraits #2, #12, and #13. Then select one of the two options beneath each picture to see a larger image.

07. In Self Portrait #2 (1628), how old was Rembrandt when he painted this picture? What expression do you see on his face?

08. In Self Portrait #12 (c. 1665-69), what explanation is there for the two circles shown behind the artist?

09. In Self Portrait #13, what two or three words would you use to describe the expression on Rembrandt's face?

THE PAINTINGS OF VERMEER
http://www.ballandclaw.com/vermeer/thumb.html
CLICK on "Thumbnails of the Paintings."

10. How many thumbnail paintings are displayed?
    [You can click on the thumbnails to display a larger image.]

11. Based on your examination of these paintings, what similarities can you find in:

    A. Subject matter? D. Colors used?

    B. Settings? E. Source of light?

    C. Mood? F. Decorative items displayed on the walls?

12. Which paintings did you like the most? Why?

CLICK on "The Paintings Sorted by Popularity"
http://www.ballandclaw.com/vermeer/pop.html

13. What was the title of the painting that was voted the most popular?

14. Why do you think Vermeer's paintings are immensely popular today (despite their obvious lack of dramatic subject matter)?

THE CHATEAU OF VERSAILLES
http://www.chateauversailles.fr/en/111_The_Grand_Apartment_And_Hall_of_Mirrors.php

- "THE HALL OF MIRRORS" / LA GALERIE DES GLACES
  Scroll down to the third paragraph (The Hall of Mirrors) and click on the illustration to the left to see a 360 degree view.

15. Describe in your own words your reaction to this room. (Move your cursor to the left or right to see all 360 degrees of the room.)

- THE GRAND APARTMENT (GRAND APPARTEMENT DU ROI)

16. What object did Louis XIV select as his emblem? (It was associated with Apollo, god of peace and arts, and was also the heavenly body which gave life to all things, regulating everything as it rose and set.)

17. Why were the rooms in this section of the palace called the Apartment of the Planets?

- THE GRAND TRIANON

http://www.chateauversailles.fr/en/121_The_Grand_Trianon.php

18. Why did the Grand Trianon Palace built by Louis XV? Why is it named the Trianon?

- THE QUEEN'S HAMLET

http://www.chateauversailles.fr/en/123_The_Queen_s_Hamlet.php

19. What was the purpose of the Queen's hamlet?

- A DAY WITH THE SUN KING

http://www.chateauversailles.fr/en/311_A_Day_with_the_Sun_King.php

20. What observation did the Duc de Saint-Simon make about the daily life of King Louis XIV, the Sun King?

21. What was the "levee" and at what time of day did it take place? Approximately how many people attended the "levee"?

22. What events took place at:

A. 11:00 am:	D. 6:00 pm:
B. 1:00 pm:	E. 10:00 pm:
C. 2:00 pm:	F. 11:30 pm

- VERSAILLES, POWER, AND AUTHORITY

http://www.chateauversailles.fr/en/312_Versailles_Power_and_Authority.php

23. In what important sense was Versailles more than just a residence for the king?

16. *THE EIGHTEENTH CENTURY: FROM ROCOCO TO REVOLUTION*

Study Questions:

ART AND MUSIC

01. What names have been applied to the eighteenth century?

    – the Age of ____________________

    – the Age of ____________________

02. Were optimism and a belief in progress characteristics of the eighteenth century?

03. What are the characteristics of the rococo style of art?

04. What was the response of rococo artists to the social needs of the 1700s?

05. For what class of people was rococo art intended?

06. Who was the first great French rococo painter (d. 1721)?

07. What two moods or emotions can be found in Watteau's *Pilgrimage to Cythera* (1717)? What is the significance of the island of Cythera? In what respect is the title inaccurate (do these people seem to be going to Cythera, or departing from Cythera)?

08. What was the subject of Watteau's *fêtes galantes*?

09. What subjects are most associated with the paintings of François Boucher (1703 – 1770)? What appears to have been the purpose of Boucher's paintings?

10. Who was a pupil of Boucher and the last of the great French rococo painters (*Love Letters*, 1773)?

11. What style was used in Balthazar Neumann's Vierzehn-heiligen (Fourteen Saints) Pilgrim Church near Bamberg, Germany?

12. Which style of art replaced rococo in the late 1700s?

13. Which art style was influenced by the excavations at Pompeii (from 1748) and the work in the 1760s and 1770s of Johannes Winckleman (the "Father of Archaeology")?

14. Which painter best represents the official art style of the French Revolution?

15. What virtue is extolled in David's *Oath of the Horatii* (1784 – 1785)?

16. In David's *Napoleon Crossing the Alps*, what message is suggested by the calm, controlled figure of Napoleon riding his wildly emotional horse? What three names are inscribed on the stones to the left?
17. Which English artist painted a series of "moral subjects" in a satirical manner?

18. What is the theme of Hogarth's *Marriage à la Mode* paintings (1743 – 1745)?

19. Who was the most important Neo-Classical sculptor from Italy?

20. In Antonio Canova's *Pauline Bonaparte Borghese as Venus* (figure 16.15)

    – what fruit is Venus holding in her left hand?

    – who awarded the prize to Venus?

    – who were the two losers?

21. Who was the most important French Neo-Classical sculptor?

22. Who was the subject of Houdon's 1788 sculpture, located in the Virginia State Capital in Richmond (figure 14.23)?

23. What is the purpose of the Pantheon (Sainte Genevieve) in Paris? Which architectural style does it represent?

24. Which architectural style is represented by Jefferson's State Capitol in Richmond, Virginia?

25. What style of music is associated with the period from the late 1700s to the early 1800s? What style became more popular in the nineteenth century?

26. Which musical figure is most associated with the change from "classical" to "romantic" music?

27. What were the characteristic qualities of ancient/classical art? How did they compare with the characteristics of Baroque art and music?

28. What form of musical composition became most popular in the classical period?

29. Which Austrian musician (1732 – 1809) is often considered the "Father of the Symphony"?

30. Who is usually considered the greatest composer (d. 1791) of the late 1700s?

31. In which opera by Mozart are the servants seen as heroes and the aristocracy as the villains?

LITERATURE

32. What was the view of human nature held by Jonathan Swift? How did it compare with the views of Diderot and Rousseau?

33. Who was the greatest English poet of the eighteenth century (the 1700s)?

34. What is the best-known book by Jonathan Swift (published in 1726)? What was the target of its satire?

35. What two aspects of man's nature are represented by Swift's Houyhnhnms and the Yahoos?

36. What seventeen-volume work (1747 – 1765) is associated with Denis Diderot? Was Diderot aiming at the minds or the hearts of his readers?

37. What position did the *Encyclopédie* take toward religion?

38. Why did Montesquieu favor establishing a system of "checks and balances" in government?

39. According to Rousseau, what had corrupted the natural goodness of humans?

40. Who is seen as the greatest French philosopher and social critic of the 1700s?

41. What institution was the target of Voltaire's *Écrasez l'infâme*? What is the English translation of this phrase?

42. What work by Voltaire ridiculed the philosophy that everything is for the best in the best of all possible worlds?

43. What is the meaning of the remark, "*Après moi le déluge*" (attributed to Louis XV, King of France, 1715 – 1774)?

44. According to the Declaration of the Rights of Man and of Citizen,

    – what was the only justification for social distinctions (paragraph one)?

    – what are the four natural and inalienable rights of man (paragraph two?

    – how is "liberty" defined (paragraph four)?

45. Who was the leader of the Reign of Terror? What was his fate?

46. What revolution in 1776 influenced the French Revolution of 1789?

47. Who was the principal author of the Declaration of Independence (1776)?

48. What is the meaning of the first paragraph of the Declaration of Independence? (Try translating it into one simple, short sentence.)

49. According to the second paragraph of the Declaration of Independence, why are governments instituted among men?

50. Review Question: What great revolution in 1789 marked the end of a period of European history?

Thought Questions:

A. Are we as optimistic as the Enlightenment about "progress," or do we feel that "the future is not what it used to be"? Why?

B. Which style do you prefer, rococo or neo-classical? Why?

C. Should "Art" also have an erotic purpose (as in many of the works of Boucher and Fragonard)? Why?

D. Do you think if we were 100% rational (like Swift's Houyhnhnms) that we would still be "human"? What else is there to being "human"?

E. Do you agree fully, somewhat, or not at all to these statements from Rousseau's *Social Contract*? Why?

  - "Man is born free, and yet we see him everywhere in chains."
  - "No citizen should be rich enough to buy another, and none so poor that he is obliged to sell himself."

F. What is your reaction to Voltaire's "I do not agree with a word you say, but I will defend to the death your right to say it"?

G. In Voltaire's *Candide*, the title character's final words are: "but we must cultivate our garden." What does this mean to you, in this <u>not</u> the best of all possible worlds?

Define or Identify:

The Enlightenment / Age of Reason
Rococo
Neo-Classical
1789: French Revolution

Significant Works To Recognize and Remember

Watteau, *Pilgrimage to Cythera*, 1717
Boucher, *Cupid a Captive*, 1754
Fragonard, *Love Letters*, 1773
Balthazar Neumann, Vierzehnheiligen Pilgrim Church, 1743 – 1772
J. L. David, *Oath of the Horatii*, 1785; *Napoleon Crossing the Alps*, 1800

Hogarth, *Marriage á la Mode* (satirical series), 1743 – 1745

Mozart, *Marriage of Figaro*, 1784

Alexander Pope, *Essay on Man*, 1734
Jonathan Swift, *Gulliver's Travels*, 1726
Denis Diderot, *Encyclopédie*, 1747 – 1765
Jean-Jacques Rousseau, *The Social Contract*, 1762
Voltaire, *Candide* ["cultivate your own garden"], 1759

Other Significant Works (Not in the textbook)

Fragonard, *The Swing*, 1766; *A Young Girl Reading,* c. 1776
Chardin, *House of Cards*, 1743
Greuze, *Broken Eggs*, 1757; *The Son Punished*, c. 1777
J.L. David, *Death of Socrates*, 1787; *Death of Marat*, 1793;
Madame Recamier, 1800
Wright of Derby, *The Experiment on a Bird in an Air Pump*, c. 1768

The proper study of mankind is man.
– Alexander Pope, *Essay on Man*

CHAPTER 16 - REVIEW

Begin by writing the title of the chapter you've just studied. Next, without looking at the text or your study guide, use your memory to recall and to list the major sections or topics covered in the chapter. Finally, check your knowledge by taking the short "Self Quiz" below.

A) CHAPTER TITLE:

B) MAJOR SECTIONS OR TOPICS:

C) SELF QUIZ # 16 – IDENTIFY THE:

01. ________________ Dominant art style of the early and mid-1700s (coming after the Baroque style).

02. ________________ First and probably the greatest French rococo painter (*Pilgrimage to Cythera*).

03. ________________ Art style that replaced rococo by the late 1700s; it was associated with the excavations at Pompeii and other classical ruins.

04. ________________ French painter best associated with Neo-Classicism, (the official art style of the French Revolution).

05. ________________ Usually considered the greatest composer of the late 1780s (*Marriage of Figaro*).

06. ________________ Massive literary work written and edited by Denis Diderot.

07. ________________ Greatest French philosopher and social critic of the 1700s ("I do not agree with a word you say, but I will defend to the death your right to say it").

08. ________________ Author of *Candide* ["Cultivate your own garden."]

09. ________________ English artist who painted a series of "moral subjects" in a satirical manner (*Marriage a la Mode*).

10. ________________ Year of the beginning of the French Revolution.

16. WEB QUESTS - THE EIGHTEENTH CENTURY

FRAGONARD

- **THE SWING, 1766**
  http://www.bc.edu/bc_org/avp/cas/his/CoreArt/art/anc_frag_swing.html

01. What is the purpose of life, as suggested by this painting?

02. Do you think the woman on the swing is aware that she is being watched? Why?

03. What does the statue on the left seem to be saying? *Click on the picture to see enlarged version.*

04. What is likely to be the fate of these aristocrats in twenty-three years? (What year will it be in twenty-three years?)

- **A YOUNG GIRL READING, 1776**
  http://www.nga.gov/cgi-bin/pimage?46020+0+0

05. What two or three words come to your mind as you look at this painting?

HOGARTH, MARRIAGE À LA MODE (c. 1743)

Hogarth is often seen as the first great English oil painter. He often reproduced his paintings in engravings that could be sold relatively cheaply. This web site contains all six paintings in the series. View the series and then answer the below questions. [There are no comments or explanations with the paintings. Look carefully at each work to answer the questions. Once in a while you may have to make a guess.]

Scene 1: <u>The Marriage Contract</u>
http://www.peterwestern.f9.co.uk/hogarth/hogarth25.html

06. Are the bride and groom paying attention to each other? Whom does the young nobleman appear to be admiring in the mirror?

07. What color mark appears to be on his neck? [This mark was considered a sign of a sexually-transmitted disease.]

08. What is being examined by the wealthy merchant (seated at the left of the round table)?

09. To what is the penniless Earl Squandor pointing with his left hand?

10. To whom is the lawyer Silvertongue (third figure from the left) paying solicitous attention?

END OF SECTION REVIEW - BAROQUE, ROCOCO, NEOCLASSICAL ART

Identify the artists of the paintings listed below:

BAROQUE ART - ITALY

01. ___________________ *David*; *St. Teresa in Ecstasy*
02. ___________________ *Calling of* St. *Matthew*
03. ___________________ *Judith and Holofemes*

BAROQUE ART - SPAIN

04. ___________________ *Las Meninas (The Maids of Honor)*

BAROQUE ART - FRANCE

05. ___________________ *Et in Arcadia Ego*
06. ___________________ *Portrait of Louis XIV*
07. ___________________ *Lamentation over Saint Sebastian*; *Repentant Magdalen*

BAROQUE ART - FLANDERS

08. ___________________ *Journey of Marie de' Medici*; *Helene Fourment*

BAROQUE ART - NETHERLANDS

09. ___________________ *Woman Reading a Letter*
10. ___________________ *The Night Watch*; *Self-Portrait*
11. ___________________ *René Descartes*

ROCOCO ART

12. ___________________ *Pilgrimage to Cythera*
13. ___________________ *Cupid a Captive*
14. ___________________ *The Swing*; *Love Letters*; *Young Girl Reading*
15. ___________________ *House of Cards*
16. ___________________ *Marriage à la Mode* (satirical series)
17. ___________________ *Broken Eggs*
18. ___________________ *Pont du Gard*; *Maison Carre at Nîmes*

NEOCLASSICAL ART

19. ___________________ *Oath of the Horatii*; *Napoleon Crossing the Alps;* *Death of Socrates*; *Death of Marat*
20. ___________________ *Experiment on a Bird in an Air Pump*

Bernini	Georges de la Tour	Robert
Boucher	Greuze	Rubens
Caravaggio	Hals	Velázquez
Chardin	Hogarth	Vermeer
David, J.L.	Poussin	Watteau
Fragonard	Rembrandt	Wright of Derby
Gentileschi	Rigaud	

17. THE ROMANTIC ERA

Study Questions:

BACKGROUND

01. What movement replaced neoclassicism in the early nineteenth century?

02. What are the principal characteristics of "romanticism"?

03. What philosopher is associated with the dialectic of thesis/antithesis/synthesis?

04. What was Karl Marx's view of the inevitability of history? In what 1848 work of his was this thought powerfully expressed? According to Marx, what forces inevitably shaped history?

05. What type of art did Marx prefer, realism or romanticism? Why?

06. What theory did Darwin use to explain the changes, disappearances, and new appearances in various species? What was the title of Darwin's first (1859) important book?

MUSIC IN THE ROMANTIC ERA

07. Who is usually regarded as the pioneer of musical romanticism? Why is his *Pathétique Piano Sonata No. 8 in c minor, Op. 13* considered an example of "romanticism" rather than "classicism"?

08. To whom was Beethoven's *Eroica* symphony intended to be dedicated? Why did he change his mind?

09. Who was the most distinguished French musical composer (1803 – 1869) during the Romantic period? What was the source of his *Fantastic Symphony*?

10. What do Chopin, Liszt, Moussorgorsky and Smetana have in common? What was the native land of each?

11. Who was the greatest Italian opera composer (*Rigoletto, Otello*) of the nineteenth century? What 1853 work of his broke new ground in the history of opera by dealing with contemporary life rather than a historical or mythological subject?

12. Who was the greatest German composer of the nineteenth century? What did he mean by *Gesamtkunstwerk*?

13. What was Richard Wagner's (1813 – 1883) most monumental opera?

What was the original source of this work?

ROMANTIC ART

14. Who was the most important Spanish artist of Romanticism?
Why are his paintings considered to be "Romantic"?

15. What was the subject of Goya's *Execution of the Madrileños on May 3, 1808 (The Third of May, 1808)*?

    - What does the central figure in white seem to be saying?
    With his arms spread out, of whom does he remind us?

    - Are the Madrileños shown as heroes? the soldiers?

    - Why are the soldiers shown in an identical position, machine-like?

16. In Goya's *The Family of Charles IV* (1800), who has been placed in the center of the painting? Which figure is a self portrait of Goya? (Why does this painting remind us of Velázquez' *The Maids of Honor*?)

17. What does Goya's *Saturn Devouring One of His Sons* suggest will be the fate of us all? [Saturn was also known as Cronus, or Time.]

18. Why does the text not apply a stylistic label to Goya's *Saturn Devouring One of His Sons*? Do great artists fit neatly into prescribed labels?

19. Who was the first important French Romantic painter?

20. In Géricault's *Raft of the Medusa* (1818),

    - How many people were crowded on to the raft (according to the text)?

    - How many actually survived?

    - In the painting, how many are shown on the raft?

    - Why are they waving?

    - How can it be explained that more than fifteen are shown on the raft at the moment a rescue ship was sighted?

21. Which French Romantic painter is remembered for *The Massacre at Chios* (1824), and *The Death of Sardanapalus* (1826)?

22. Match the below characteristics of nineteenth-century Romanticism with the appropriate paintings:

a. emotion	c. personal feelings
b. love of Nature	d. love of exotic places

_______ *Sleep of Reason Produces Monsters*
_______ *Raft of the Medusa*
_______ *Death of Sardanapalus*
_______ *The Hay Wain*

23. Which art style ("ism") came after romanticism and emphasized the everyday events of this world rather than the exotic or distant past?

24. Which style of art is associated with Honoré Daumier and Gustave Courbet?

25. Who was the most important German painter of the Romantic period? Why are his works, such as *Cloister Graveyard in the Snow* (1810) considered "romantic"?

26. What two English painters are known for their portrayal of Nature?

 - *The Hay Wain* (1821):

 - *The Slave Ship* (1840):

LITERATURE

27. Who was the leader of the German literary movement known as *Sturm und Drang* (Storm and Stress)? How would members of this movement feel about neoclassical ideas of reason, order, and balance?

28. Who was the founder of the Romantic movement in English poetry?

29. Which English poet saw his work as "emotion recollected in tranquillity"?

30. How was the popularity of the nineteenth-century novel related to the rise of an educated public eager for both instruction and entertainment in their fiction?

31. What was the subject of Victor Hugo's *Les Miserables*?

32. What important French Realist novelist (1821 – 1880) described the banal life of bourgeois (middle-class) Emma Bovary?

33. Who was the greatest (especially in quantity) of the French Realist novelists? What general title is given to his ninety novels and stories?

34. Why did George Sand (1804 – 1876) find it easy to defend women's rights and to attack male privilege?

35. Which novel is considered to be the most important work (1863 – 1869) of Russian Realist fiction? Who was its author?

35. Who was the greatest English Realist novelist of the nineteenth century? Which of his novels criticized the treatment of the poor in workhouses?

AMERICA

37. What work of Ralph Waldo Emerson in 1837 called for the development of a national literature for Americans?

38. What was Henry David Thoreau's greatest work? What was its subject?

39. Who was America's first great poet? What was his most important work (1855)?

40. What book by Herman Melville is often considered "the greatest of all American works of fiction"?

41. What was the general subject of the paintings of the Hudson River School and of Winslow Homer?

42. What name ("ism") was given to painters like Martin J. Heade (*Lake George*) who achieved a photographic realism in their works?

Thought Questions:

A. Why would "survival of the fittest" be good for the human race? How would you define "fittest"? Why would anyone object to "survival of the fittest"? Are there other approaches for people not able to survive their environment, for example, improving the environment? Could improving the environment include the educational environment as well as the physical environment?

B. The nineteenth-century novel was popular because it provided both entertainment and instruction. Do you think both entertainment and instruction are important parts of contemporary novels? of good theater? of good movies? of good teaching?

C. Should Captain Ahab's single-minded pursuit of revenge against evil Moby Dick be seen as a form of madness deservedly resulting in tragedy? Why?

Define or Identify:

Romanticism (Characteristics)
Hegel: Synthesis, thesis, antithesis
Wordsworth – English Romanticism
    ("emotion recollected in tranquillity"; love of nature)
Musical Nationalism: Liszt, Chopin, Moussorgsky, Smetana
gesamtkunstwerk (Wagner)
Realism
    Art: Courbet, Daumier
    Literature: Dickens, Flaubert, Balzac

Significant Works To Recognize and Remember

Karl Marx, *Communist Manifesto*, 1848
Charles Darwin, *Origin of Species,* 1859
Beethoven, Symphony No. 3 "*Eroica,*" 1804
Berlioz, *Fantastic Symphony*, 1830
Verdi, *La Traviata*, 1853; *Otello*, 1887
Richard Wagner, *Ring of the Nibelung*, 1876
Goya, *The Third of May, 1808*, 1814; *Sleep of Reason Produces Monsters,* 1798; *Saturn Devouring One of His Sons*, c. 1821
Géricault, *Raft of the Medusa*, 1824
Delacroix, *Massacre at Chios*, 1824; *Death of Sardanapalus*, 1826
Friedrich, *Cloister Graveyard in the Snow*, 1810
Courbet, *The Artist's Studio*, 1855
Constable, *Hay Wain,* 1821
Turner, *Slave Ship*, 1840

Goethe, *Sufferings of Young Werther*, 1774; *Faust*, 1808-1832
Dickens, *Oliver Twist*, 1838; *Hard Times*, 1854
Gustave Flaubert, *Madame Bovary*, 1857
Balzac, *The Human Comedy*, 1829 – 1850
Tolstoy, *War and Peace*, 1863 – 1869
Emerson, "The American Scholar," 1837
Thoreau, *Walden*, 1854
Whitman, *Leaves of Grass*, 1855
Melville, *Moby Dick*, 1851

Imagination abandoned by reason produces impossible monsters;
united with her, she is the mother of the arts and the source of their wonders.
– Goya

Other Important Works (Not in the textbook)

Goya, *Disasters of War*, 1814
Delacroix, *Liberty Leading the People*, 1831
Blake, *Newton,* 1795; *Nebuchadnezzar,* 1795
Turner, *The Fighting Téméraire,* 1838; *Rain, Steam, Speed,* 1844
Friedrich, *Cross in the Mountains*, 1808;
Wanderer Above the Mists, 1818
Millet, *The Gleaners*, 1857; *The Angelus*, 1857
Rosa Bonheur, *Plowing in the Nivernais*, 1850; *The Horse Fair*, c. 1855
Frederick Edwin Church, *View of the Andes*, 1854

Daumier, *Third-class Carriage*, c. 1862
Courbet, *The Stone Breakers*, 1849; *Funeral at Ornans*, 1849

Thomas Cole, *The Oxbow /The Connecticut River Near Northampton*), 1836; *Course of Empire*, 1836
Albert Bierstadt, *The Rocky Mountains, Lander's Peak*, 1863
Winslow Homer, *Snap the Whip*, 1872; *The Gulf Stream*, 1899

CHAPTER 17 - REVIEW

Begin by writing the title of the chapter you've just studied. Next, without looking at the text or your study guide, use your memory to recall and to list the major sections or topics covered in the chapter. Finally, check your knowledge by taking the short "Self Quiz" below.

A) CHAPTER TITLE:

B) MAJOR SECTIONS OR TOPICS:

C) SELF QUIZ # 17 – IDENTIFY THE:

01. ______________ Style of art associated with emotion and a love of nature.

02. ______________ Pioneer German composer of musical romanticism (*Pathétique Symphony; Fidelio*).

03. ______________ Greatest Italian composer of the nineteenth century (*Rigoletto, Otello*).

04. ______________ Nineteenth-century German composer (*The Ring of the Niebelung*), advocate of *Gesamtkunstwerk*.

05. ______________ Most important Spanish artist of Romanticism (*The Sleep of Reason Produces Monsters; Third of May, 1808*).

06. ______________ First important French painter of Romanticism (*Raft of the Medusa*, 1818).

07. ______________ Most important German painter of Romanticism (*Cloister Graveyard in the Snow*).

08. ______________ Important English Romantic painter known for his stormy, turbulent scenes of Nature (*The Slave Ship* [also *The Fighting Téméraire*, and *Rain, Steam, Speed.*])

09. ______________ Style of art most associated with Honoré Daumier, Gustave Courbet [and Jean François Millet].

10. ______________ Greatest nineteenth-century English novelist of Realism (*Oliver Twist*).

11. ______________ American Transcendentalist and author of *Walden*.

17. WEB QUESTS - THE ROMANTIC ERA

CASPER DAVID FRIEDRICH
http://www.ibiblio.org/wm/paint/auth/friedrich/

01. What is the name of the first image on the home page of this site?

02. At the bottom of this site, there are six thumbnail images from the "Friedrich page" of the Web Museum. Which one do you like the most? Why? [*Click on the "thumbnail" for a larger image.*]

GOYA -THE "BLACK PAINTINGS" FROM "QUINTA DEL SORDA"
http://www.artchive.com/galleries/goya/notes.html#paintings

03. What is the meaning of "Quinta del sordo"?

04. What type of images decorate the "Quinta del sordo"?

05. How many images were painted on the walls of this cottage?

06. Where are these images displayed now?

07. (*Enter the room by clicking on the door.*) Describe the image to the left of the center window.

08. (*Click on the stairs to go upstairs.*) View all four walls and select the painting that interests you the most. Describe the painting and explain why it interested you.

GOYA, *Caprichos [Caprices]*, #14 and #16
http://www.wesleyan.edu/dac/imag/1946/00D1/0040/1946-D1-40-14-m.html
http://www.wesleyan.edu/dac/imag/1946/00D1/0040/1946-D1-40-16-m.html

09. "What a Sacrifice" (#14) – What is being sacrificed?

10. "For Heaven's Sake; and it was Her Mother" (#16) – what does this say about "not seeing" those who beg?

BLAKE - NEWTON (1795)
http://www.princeton.edu/~his291/Newton.html

11. On what is the great scientist Isaac Newton concentrating his attention?

12. Is the result of Newton's work produced by the mind and reason or by the heart and faith?

WILLIAM BLAKE, "LONDON," 1793 (SONGS OF INNOCENCE AND EXPERIENCE)
http://www.tate.org.uk/britain/exhibitions/blakeinteractive/works/songs_08.html#
Look at Blake's illustrated manuscript by moving your cursor over the page to see the pop-up notes. Then, listen to a recording of the poem by going to the link just below the poem and selecting MP3 or Real Audio. Finally, think about the work by reading the "Summary" and "Analysis" at the bottom of the page.

13. After reading, listening, and thinking, answer the below questions:

    a) What does Blake see in every face (marks of _____, marks of _____)?

    b) What does he mean by "mind-forg'd manacles"?

    c) What are two meanings of the "youthful Harlot's curse"?

    d) How does the curse lead to a "marriage-hearse"?

"CHIMNEY SWEEPER" (1789)
CLICK on the link "Chimney Sweeper" in the list of works located just above the summary. Once again, look, listen, and think about the work by using the links provided beneath the illustration.

14. After reading and listening to *The Chimney Sweeper,* answer these questions:

    a) What does the child mean to say when he says "weep, weep"?

    b) How old were boys when they were sold to become chimney sweeps?

    c) What is the real meaning of the last line, "So if all do their duty, they need not fear harm."

THOREAU - WALDEN
http://xroads.virginia.edu/~HYPER/WALDEN/toc.html
Click on Chapter "I. Economy" and read the paragraphs 1, 4, 9, and 19.

15. How long did Thoreau live on the shore of Walden Pond? [Paragraph 1]

16. Why was it a misfortune "to have inherited farms, houses, barns, cattle, and farming tools"? [Paragraph 4]

17. What kind of lives (quiet ___________) do most people lead? [Paragraph 9]

18. "The so called comforts of life, are not only not indispensable, but _________ ________ to the elevation of mankind." [Paragraph 19]

ROSA BONHEUR
http://www.albrightknox.org/ArtStart/Bonheur.html

19. Who was the most famous woman artist of the first three quarters of the nineteenth century?

20. Since it was not possible for a woman to attend the official schools of art at this time (that right was not granted until 1897), who served as her instructor?

21. What was “radical” about Bonheur's personal life?

22. What was her most famous painting (1853)?

18. TOWARD THE MODERN ERA: 1870 – 1914

Study Questions:

INTRODUCTION

01. In Paris, what name was given to the period 1870 – 1914?

02. Who was the author of *Thus Spake Zarathustra* (1883 – 1892)?

03. What was Friedrich Nietzsche's view of the condition of Western civilization in the 1880s and 1890s? Did he accept the view of those who saw it as the *Belle Époque*?

04. What was Nietzsche's view of Christianity? of democracy? What did he believe should be the only valid life force for the *ubermensch* ("overperson")?

THE VISUAL ARTS

05. What five new movements in art appeared between 1870 and 1914?

I __ __ __ __ __ __ __ __ __ __ __ __ __
P __ __ __ - __ __ __ __ __ __ __ __ __ __ __ __ __
F __ __ __ __ __ __
E __ __ __ __ __ __ __ __ __ __ __ __ __
C __ __ __ __ __

06. Which European city was the center of artistic activity in the nineteenth century?

07. Why were Parisians shocked by Édouard Manet's *Déjeuner sur l'Herbe* (*Luncheon on the Grass*)? Were people influenced by Manet's use of contemporary clothing, which set the scene in the present rather than in the distant past? What is the effect of having the woman gazing directly at the viewer, unabashed and with tranquillity?

08. How "realistic" is it to have broad, flat colors on a canvas? Did this painting influence the development of modern art, so much of which consists of "flat colors on a canvas"?

09. Who is seen as the "father of Impressionism"? What painting (1872) is responsible for this title?

10. Instead of the "realism" of form, what type of "realism" did the paintings of the impressionists emphasize?

11. *In Red Boats at Argenteuil*, does Monet's real subject seem to be the boats, or light and color? What would be the real subject in his series of paintings of *Water Lilies*? (of his other series of paintings such as *Haystacks, Rouen Cathedral* or the *Houses of Parliament*?)

12. In what way can Monet's *Water Lilies* be considered "abstract art"? What is meant by "abstract art"? What does the word *abstract* mean?

13. How do the paintings of Auguste Renoir express the spirit of the *Belle Époque*?

14. What does Renoir's *Le Moulin de la Galette* (1876) suggest about the pleasantness possible for people living in cities such as Paris in the 1870s?

15. What does Edgar Degas' *The Rehearsal* (1874) suggest about the "glamorous" world of the ballet?

16. What were the usual subjects of the paintings of Mary Cassatt? As a woman, was she as free to paint the same subjects as Monet or other impressionists?

17. What was the influence of Mary Cassatt on the popularity of impressionist painting in America?

18. Review Question: Which of the Impressionists is best remembered for

    – pleasant, happy pictures of people enjoying themselves?

    – unusual perspectives/vantage points of scenes, often of the ballet?

    – paintings of a mother and child?

19. Who was the greatest sculptor of the *Belle Époque*?

20. What expression do you see on Balzac's face in Rodin's *Monument to Balzac*? Is your perception influenced by looking up at the face?

21. What was distinctive about the technique of painting used by Georges Seurat in his *Sunday Afternoon on the Island of La Grande Jatte*?

22. To which post-impressionist would the term "pointillism" be best applied?

23. Which post-impressionist left France and its civilization for the attractions of Tahiti (and "barbarism")?

24. Which painting of Paul Gauguin tried to blend Western spiritual values with the simple beauty of primitive Polynesian life?

25. According to the text, who was the greatest post-impressionist painter? Why?

26. What was revolutionary about the art of Paul Cézanne?

27. In contrast to the realism sought by painters in the six hundred years since Giotto, what was Cézanne trying to achieve in his paintings?

28. What is it about Cézanne's *Mont Saint-Victoire* that makes it not realistic? What geometric shapes are apparent? How can Cézanne be seen as a predecessor to Cubist and Abstract Art?

29. Who was the most important Dutch post-impressionist artist?

30. Which painting of Van Gogh did he describe as "one of the ugliest I have ever done" and the subject as "a place where one can ruin oneself, go mad, or commit a crime"?

31. What expression do you see on the face of Van Gogh's *Portrait of Dr. Gachet* (1890)?

32. Of which post-impressionist artist can it be said that he painted what he <u>felt</u> more than what he <u>saw</u>?

33. Around 1905, what new style of art appeared in France? in Germany?

34. Who was the leading spirit of Fauvism?

35. What was "fauvism"? What was it about the use of color and form in Matisse's *The Joy of Life* (1905) or *The Red Studio* (1911) that would cause critics to call him a "wild beast"?

36. Which Norwegian artist (1863-1944) is considered the forerunner of expressionist art? What is his best known work (1893) of art? How does this painting relate to the alienation and loneliness felt by many people then and now?

MUSIC

37. What is the purpose of a "symphonic poem" (or "tone poem") such as Richard Strauss' *Don Juan* (1886)?

38. Which two French composers are associated with impressionism in music?

39. What was the reaction of the Paris audience in 1913 to the first performance of Stravinsky's *Rite of Spring*? Why?

40. Which Austrian composer (1874 – 1951) began in 1908 to write atonal music (music avoiding traditional chords and harmonies)?

LITERATURE

41. According to Sigmund Freud, what factors other than reason and logic, influence human behavior?

42. What Russian novelist (1831 – 1881) was able to combine both realism and psychological understanding in his *Crime and Punishment* (1866)? Why does Raskolnikov eventually go to the police and confess his crime?

43. What Russian dramatist (1860 – 1904) showed the emptiness of life in plays such as *The Three Sisters*?

44. What French author (1871 – 1922) is associated with "stream-of-consciousness" writing? What is his best known work?

45. What does the text mean when it says "memory is our most important weapon against death"?

46. Who was the important Norwegian dramatist (1828 – 1906) of social realism? What was the final sound in his play *A Doll's House* (1879)? Why would Nora decide to leave her doll's house? What was Nora's response to the statement "one doesn't sacrifice one's honor for love's sake"?

47. Who was the most important English-speaking dramatist (1856 – 1950) of social realism and protest?

48. In Kate Chopin's *The Awakening* (1899), what did Edna do to escape the meaningless relationship she had with her husband and the boring life she faced every day?

Thought Questions:

A. Parisians were shocked by Édouard Manet's *Déjeuner sur l'Herbe* (*Luncheon on the Grass*). Why do you think they were not upset by paintings of classical and mythological nudes?

B. What thoughts or feelings do you have in viewing Van Gogh's *Starry Night*?

C. How is our "remembrance of things past" a way of keeping things "alive" (and therefore a weapon against death)? As long as a person is still in someone's memory, is that person still "alive"?

D. Is one purpose of this course is to keep alive our culture's "remembrance of things past"? What would be another purpose?

We are all in the gutter, but some of us are looking at the stars.
– Oscar Wilde, *Lady Windermere's Fan* (1892)

Define or Identify:

Belle Époque
Impressionism
Post-Impressionism
Expressionism
Fauvism
Tone Poem
Schoenberg, atonal music: twelve-tone technique

Significant Works To Recognize and Remember

Nietzsche, *Thus Spake Zarathustra* (*ubermensch*), 1883 – 1892
Édouard Manet, *Luncheon on the Grass*, 1863
Claude Monet, *Impression: Sunrise*, 1872; *Water Lilies*, 1920
Renoir, *Moulin de la Galette*, 1876
Edgar Degas, *The Dance Class* 1874
Mary Cassatt, *Mother and Child*, 1889
Rodin, *The Kiss*, 1886; *Balzac*, 1898

Seurat, *Sunday Afternoon on Island of La Grande Jatte,* 1884 – 1886
(pointillism)
Gauguin, *Ia Orana Maria*, 1891
Cézanne, *Mont Sainte-Victoire*, 1906
Vincent van Gogh, *Night Cafe*, 1888; *Starry Night*, 1889;

Edvard Munch, *The Scream,* 1893
Matisse, *The Joy of Life*, 1906
Emil Nolde, *The Last Supper*, 1909

Richard Strauss, *Don Juan,* 1886; *Till Eulenspeigel,* 1895; *Salome*, 1905
Claude Debussy, *La Mer*, 1905
Stravinsky, *The Rite of Spring*, 1913

Marcel Proust, *Remembrance of Things Past*, 1913-1927
(stream-of-consciousness)
Ibsen, *A Doll's House*, 1879
Kate Chopin, *The Awakening*, 1899

Other Important Works (Not in the textbook)

Manet, *Olympia*, 1863
Monet, *Gare St. Lazare*, 1877; *Haystacks* series, 1891; *Rouen Cathedral* series, 1894; *Houses of Parliament*, 1899 – 1901
Renoir, *The Boating Party,* 1881
Morisot, *The Cradle / Le Berceau*, 1874

Van Gogh, *Potato Eaters*, 1885; *Self Portraits*
Rousseau ("Le Douanier"), *Tropical Storm with a Tiger [Surprise!],* 1891; *The Sleeping Gypsy*, 1897

Henry O. Tanner, *The Banjo Player*, 1893

Derain, *London Bridge*, 1906

Tiffany, *Wisteria Lamp*, 1902 (*Art Nouveau*)
Klimt, *The Kiss*, 1908 (*Jugenstil*)

Rodin, *The Thinker, 1880*; *The Gate of Hell*, 1880 – 1917; *The Hand of God*, 1902 – 1916

Brancusi, *Sleeping Muse*, 1909; *The Kiss*, 1910; *Bird*, 1911

George Bernard Shaw, *Candida*, 1895; *Major Barbara*, 1905; *Pygmalion*, 1912
Oscar Wilde, *Lady Windermere's Fan*, 1892; *The Importance of Being Earnest*, 1895
Anton Chekhov, *Three Sisters*, 1899; *The Cherry Orchard*, 1904
August Strindberg, *The Father*, 1887; *Dance of Death*, 1901

CHAPTER 18 - REVIEW

Begin by writing the title of the chapter you've just studied. Next, without looking at the text or your study guide, use your memory to recall and to list the major sections or topics covered in the chapter. Finally, check your knowledge by taking the short "Self Quiz" below.

A) CHAPTER TITLE:

B) MAJOR SECTIONS OR TOPICS:

C) SELF QUIZ # 18 – IDENTIFY THE:

01. ______________ Name given in Paris to the period from 1870 to 1914.

02. ______________ "Father of Impressionism" (*Impression: Sunrise*).

03. ______________ French Impressionist who loved painting happy pictures of people enjoying themselves in Paris (*Le Moulin de la Galette, 1876*).

04. ______________ Most important American Impressionist; she painted *Mother and Child* in 1889.

05. ______________ Greatest sculptor of the period 1870 to 1924; *Monument to Balzac; The Kiss.*

06. ______________ Painter of *Mont Saint-Victoire*; his interest in showing the geometric shapes he found in nature make him a predecessor to the Cubists.

07. ______________ Best known Dutch post-impressionist artist (*The Starry Night, The Night Cafe*).

08. ______________ Post-Impressionist of Tahitians (*Ia Orana Maria*, 1891).

09. ______________ French term applied in 1905 to Matisse (the painter of *The Joy of Life*, *The Red Studio*) and other "wild beasts."

10. ______________ Most famous work of art (1893) by the Norwegian expressionist Edvard Munch.

11. ______________ Important play dealing with women's rights in 1879 by the Norwegian dramatist Henrik Ibsen; at the end Nora closes the door to her home.

18. WEB QUESTS - TOWARD THE MODERN ERA

VAN GOGH'S VAN GOGHS:
MASTERPIECES FROM THE VAN GOGH MUSEUM, AMSTERDAM
http://www.nga.gov/exhibitions/gogh/html/nonplug/room1-main.htm
Take a virtual tour of "Van Gogh's Van Goghs: Masterpieces from the Van Gogh Museum, Amsterdam." This exhibition was on view at the National Gallery in Washington, D.C., and was revised as an online tour in 2005. Select the "Van Gogh Tour (no special requirements.)"

CLICK on "Real Audio" to listen to a two-minute introduction to Van Gogh.

01. What did you learn from listening to the introductory talk, for example, how many of Van Gogh's letters survive?

- ***THE POTATO EATERS*** (Nuenen, April, 1885)

CLICK on "The Potato Eaters" in the left frame. Then CLICK on the painting that appears in the center of the room. Next, CLICK on "Real Audio" to hear a one-minute talk on the painting. When the talk begins, CLICK on the image of the painting to see a full-screen image of it while listening to the talk.

02. Did Van Gogh intend for this to be a sentimental or realistic view of peasants? Would you describe this as a work of Romanticism or Realism? Why?

03. Why did he send this particular work to his brother Theo?

04. What are these peasants experiencing at dinner every night that most American families may experience only once or twice a week?

- ***SELF-PORTRAIT AS AN ARTIST*** (Paris: 1887 – 1888)

Return to the first page, and CLICK on "Self Portraits." CLICK on the painting that appears in the center of the room. Next, CLICK on "Real Audio" to hear a one-minute talk on the painting. When the talk begins, CLICK on the image of the painting to see a full-screen image of it while listening to the talk.

05. According to the letter Van Gogh wrote to his sister Wil, "It isn't an easy job to paint one's self. It is to be different from a ____________." What would be the difference?

- ***THE YELLOW HOUSE (Arles, 1888)***

Return to the first page, and CLICK on "The Yellow House." Then CLICK on the arrow to the right of the picture. Now CLICK on the painting that appears in the center of the room. Then CLICK on "Real Audio" to hear a one-minute talk on the painting. When the talk begins, CLICK on the image of the painting to see a full-screen image of it while listening to the talk.

06. What was Van Gogh's goal in moving to the South of France and renting this house?

- ***THE BED ROOM* (Arles, 1888)**

CLICK on the arrow to the left of the painting. Then *CLICK on the painting that appears in the center of the room. Next, CLICK on "Real Audio" to hear a one-minute talk on the painting. When the talk begins, CLICK on the image of the painting to see a full-screen image of it while listening to the talk.*

07. What incident caused Gauguin to hastily leave Van Gogh's yellow house in Arles?

RODIN, THE HAND OF GOD
http://www.musee-rodin.fr/smarb-e.htm#dieu-e

08. What artistic theory about sculpture did Rodin set forth in 1890?

09. What surprising information did you discover about Rodin's work as a sculptor? What word would more accurately describe Rodin's work as a "sculptor"?

10. What is God holding in His hand?

ART NOUVEAU: 1890 – 1914
http://www.nga.gov/feature/nouveau/exhibit_audio.htm#
Look specifically at the below works and then listen to a Real Audio commentary for each by clicking on the Real Audio ("play audio segment") link provided.

- **Victor Horta, *Tassel House, Brussels, Belgium,* 1893**

11. Why is this house important in the history of Art Nouveau architecture?

- **Hector Guimard, *Entrance to the Métropolitain,* c. 1900**

12. What event in Paris coincided with the opening of many of Guimard Metro entrances?

- **Louis Comfort Tiffany, *Jack-in-the-Pulpit vase,* c. 1902**

13. What word meaning "handwrought" did Tiffany to his new type of blown glass?

HENRY O. TANNER, THE BANJO PLAYER, 1893
http://www.angelfire.com/me2/zoneart/hotanner.html

14. What is the lesson of this painting? What stereotype did it contradict?

15. Why did Tanner move to Paris in 1894 and abandon painting pictures of African Americans and turn instead to biblical subjects?

GAUGUIN, WHERE DO WE COME FROM? WHAT ARE WE? WHERE ARE WE GOING? (1897)
http://www.mfa.org/handbook/portrait.asp?id=272&s=6
Listen to the commentary by clicking on the triangle to the left of the Real Audio icon. Do not click on the Real Audio icon; it will bring you to an advertisement.

16. A. Which work did Gauguin consider to be his masterpiece? Where was it painted?

    B. In this 1897 work, what is represented by the three women and child on the right? the central group of figures? the old woman at the left?

    C. Why did Gauguin not intend the meaning of this work to be absolutely clear?

GUSTAV KLIMT, THE KISS, 1907 – 1908
http://www.artchive.com/artchive/K/klimt/kiss.jpg.html
CLICK on the picture for a larger image.

17. A. On what does she appear to be leaning?

    B. What is in the space behind the couple?

    C. Does the couple appear to be aware of their surroundings? What are they aware of?

CONSTANTIN BRANCUSI
- THE KISS, 1907, 1912
http://www.eyeconart.net/history/sculpture.htm

18. Which version do you prefer, the 1907 or the 1912? Why?

19. *Scroll down the page to "Site Sculpture/ Environmental Sculpture" to see Claes Oldenburg's, Clothespin (also in Philadelphia).* How is Oldenburg's *Clothespin* similar to Brancusi's *The Kiss*?

- *MAIASTRA*, 1912 (?), *BIRD IN SPACE*, 1932 – 1940
http://www.guggenheimcollection.org/site/artist_works_22_0.html
Click on these two works to see a larger image and scroll down to read the text information. Clicking on the image again will produce an even larger image.

20. Compare the images for *Maiastra* and *Bird in Space*. Which is more abstract? Which one do you prefer? Why?

21. What does the word *maiastra* mean in Brancusi's native Romanian language?

22. According to the commentary below the image, *Bird in Space*, "stripped of individualizing features communicates the notion of __________ ________ rather than describing the appearance of a particular bird".

19. *INDIA, CHINA, AND JAPAN: FROM THE MEDIEVAL TO THE MODERN WORLD*

Study Questions:

INDIA

01. What city was the first center of Muslim power in India?

02. In what year was the Delhi Sultanate established?

03. Who was the founder of the Mughal Empire in India in 1526? Who became the most powerful ruler (1542 – 1605) of the Mughal Empire?

04. What was the attitude of Akbar toward the diverse religions in his empire?

05. What new language (a blending of Hindi, Arabic, and Persian) was created by the scholars of Akbar?

06. What three innovations from Arabic architecture were introduced by Muslim architects into Mughal architecture?

07. What is the most famous of all Mughal buildings (1632 – 1649)? Why did Shah Jehan order the construction of this building?

08. How does the subject matter of Mughal painting differ from earlier Hindu and Buddhist art?

09. How did Mughal artists feel about the use of calligraphy in their miniature paintings?

10. What was the status of religious tolerance in the Mughal Empire by the time of Aurangzeb (1618 – 1707) and the end of Mughal rule in India?

11. What British company ruled much of India from the 1600s and 1700s?

12. Who was the best known leader of Indian nationalism (from c. 1915 to 1948)?

13. What was the principle of resistance (*Satyagraha*) adopted by Gandhi?

14. Although born a Brahmin, Gandhi held what attitude on the caste system of traditional Hinduism?

15. What two independent countries emerged in 1948 from the subcontinent of India? Which one was predominantly Hindu? Predominantly Muslim?

CHINA

16. What dynasty controlled China from 1368 to 1644? from 1644 to 1911?

17. What British company arrived in China in 1689?

18. Who was the most important Chinese philosopher during the Ming Dynasty?

19. What two literary genres became popular during the Ming Dynasty?

20. What novel by Wu Ch'eng-en (c. 1510 – 1580) has a main character named Tripitaka who represents a kind of Chinese "Everyman"?

21. What character in *Monkey* represents the ingenuity of human intelligence?

22. During the Ming Dynasty, what was a popular subject for painters such as Shen Zhou?

23. Which of the decorative arts is often included in the landscape paintings of the Ming Dynasty (such as Figures 19.6 and 19.7)?

24. What city was reconstructed in the early 1400s to serve as the Imperial capital of the Ming Dynasty?

25. What was the name of the section of Beijing containing the residence of the emperor? the main government offices?

26. In which direction faced the chief buildings of the Forbidden City and the Imperial City? Why? In which direction was the main entranceway, the Gate of Heavenly Peace ("Tiananmen Square")?

27. What dynasty came to rule China from the early 1600s to 1911?

28. Why did most Chinese view the Qing rulers as foreigners? Where did the Qing rulers come from? What was the general attitude of Qing rulers toward European religious and commercial expansionism?

29. In the early 1800s, what product from India did the British insist they had a right to sell or exchange for goods in China? What was the result when the Chinese tried to block the introduction of this product?

30. What was the result on Western influence in China with the suppression of the Boxer Rebellion of 1900 – 1901?

31. In what year was a republic established in China? Who was its first important leader?

32. Who were the two most important political leaders of China after the death of Sun Yat-sen?

33. What was the purpose of art produced under the communist rule of Mao Tse-tung, for example, the 1965 sculptured scene of rent collection with peasants kneeling before their masters [Fig. 19.15]?

JAPAN

34. What city replaced Nara and served as the capital of Japan from the 700s to 1185?

35. What was the name of the religion native to Japan?

36. What did Shintoism believe about the importance of worshipping spirits of nature? About worshipping the ruling emperor and his ancestors?

37. What was the importance of Lady Murasaki Shikibu's *The Tale of Genji*?

38. What comparison does *The Tale of Genji* make between the aesthetic sensibilities of the aristocratic elite and the lives of ordinary people?

39. What is the meaning of the word *samurai*?

40. What was the meaning of the title *Seiitaishogun*? What was the shortened version of this title?

41. What invading foreigners were stopped in 1274 and 1281?

42. What new technology introduced by Portuguese traders undercut the traditional *samurai* fighting style?

43. What new capital was created in 1603 by the Tokugawa Shogunate?

44. What is the present-day name for the city of Edo?

45. In the early 1800s, who was the most famous artist working in woodcuts?

46. What is the best known woodcut of Hokusai [Fig. 19.20]?

47. Who was the greatest poet (1644 – 1694) of the Edo period?

48. What important Japanese verse form (consisting of three lines of five, seven, and five syllables) was developed by Basho?

49. What does *haiku* try to achieve in poetry that is similar to one of the goals of Zen Buddhism?

50. In Zen Buddhism, how important are sacred texts?

51. How did the subject matter of *no* theater compare with the new dramas of *kabuki*?

52. In 1853, what event thrust Japan into contact with western powers?

53. After coming into power in 1867, what was the attitude of the new emperor and new Meiji government toward industrialization and modernization?

54. What was the result of the Meiji reforms upon Japan in the Russo-Japanese War of 1905?

POSTSCRIPT: A NOTE ON ASIAN FILM

55. Who is the best known

    a) Chinese film director?

    b) Indian film director?

    c) Japanese filmmaker?

56. What are two of the important films of Zhang Yimou?

57. What is the general title for Satyajit Ray's famous trilogy of films (*Pather Panchali*, *Aparajito*, and *The World of Apu*)? Who composed and played the background music for *The Apu Trilogy*?

58. What was the first film of Akira Kurosawa to catch international attention?

59. What 1954 film by Kurosawa has been listed as one of the ten greatest films of all time? What was the name of Kurosawa's 1985 version of Shakespeare's *King Lear*?

Thought Questions:

A. The Taj Mahal is often considered one of the most beautiful buildings in the India. What do you think is the most beautiful building in America? in your home town? Why is it beautiful to you?

B. If the films of Satyajit Ray, Zhang Yimou, and Akira Kurosawa are great films, why are they not shown in most U.S. movie theaters or presented on television?

In a gentle way, you can shake the world.
– Mahatma Gandhi (1869 – 1948)

Define or Identify:

India
- Mughal Empire
  - Akbar
- Gandhi

China
- Ming Dynasty (1368 – 1644)
  - Beijing
  - Wu Ch'eng-en (c. 1510 – 1580), *Monkey*
- Qing Dynasty
  - Opium War, 1839 – 1840
- Revolution of 1911
- Peoples Republic of China, 1949
  - Mao Tse-tung

Japan
- Shintoism
- Kyoto
- *Samurai*
- *Shogun*
- Meiji Restoration (of imperial government) – Edo / Tokyo
- Basho, *haiku*
- Zen Buddhism

Asian Filmmakers
- Satyajit Ray, *The World of Apu*, 1955 – 1958
- Zhang Yimou, *The Story of Qui Ju*, 1992; *To Live*, 1994
- Akira Kurosawa, *Rashomon*, 1950; *The Seven Samurai*, 1954; *Ran*, 1985

Significant Works To Recognize and Remember

Taj Mahal, Agra, India, 1632 – 1649
Shen Zhou, *Poet on a Mountaintop*, c. 1500
Murasawaki, *Tale of Genji*, c. 1001 – 1015
Hokusai, *The Great Wave,* 1831

Other Important Works (Not in the textbook)

Ukiyo-e – "Floating World"
Kitagawa Utamaro, *Ten Physiognomic Types of Women*, 1794
Hiroshige, *The Tokaido Fifty-Three Stations*, 1834

CHAPTER 19 - REVIEW

Begin by writing the title of the chapter you've just studied. Next, without looking at the text or your study guide, use your memory to recall and to list the major sections or topics covered in the chapter. Finally, check your knowledge by taking the short "Self Quiz" below.

A) CHAPTER TITLE:

B) MAJOR SECTIONS OR TOPICS:

C) SELF QUIZ # 19 – IDENTIFY THE:

01. ________________ Most famous of Mughal buildings, located in Agra, India.

02. ________________ Greatest leader (1542 – 1605) of the Mughal Empire; a scholar and patron of the arts, he practiced religious toleration.

03. ________________ Nationalist leader in twentieth-century India; he advocated nonviolent civil disobedience.

04. ________________ Mongol city rebuilt and retained as a capital by the Ming Dynasty, and still the capital of China today.

05. ________________ Decorative writing used in combination with paintings of the Ming Dynasty, e.g., Shen Zhou's, *Poet on a Mountaintop*, c. 1500.

06. ________________ Native religion of Japan; it emphasized worship of Nature and of the Emperor and his ancestors.

07. ________________ Most famous novel of early Japan; it was written by the Lady Murasaki (c. 980 – 1030).

08. ________________ Japanese word for professional warrior.

09. ________________ Japanese form of Buddhism which emphasizes the importance of enlightenment from sudden insight.

10. ________________ Most famous painting of Hokusai; [one of his *Thirty-Six Views of Mt. Fuji*, c. 1831].

19. WEB QUESTS - INDIA, CHINA, AND JAPAN

TAJ MAHAL: A TRIBUTE TO BEAUTY
http://www.angelfire.com/in/myindia/tajmahal.html

01. What were the words used by Rabindranath Tagore to describe the Taj Mahal? ("___ ____________ on the cheek of time.")

02. What is the meaning of the words "Taj Mahal"?

03. Who was the Mughal Emperor responsible for the building of the Taj Mahal?

04. What woman was honored by the building of the Taj Mahal?

05. How many children did Banu Begum, also known as Mumtaz Mahal ("Chosen of the Palace"), have before she died?

06. While still alive, what four promises did Mumtaz Mahal extract from her husband, Shah Jahan? Which two of these promises did he keep?

07. What is the purpose of the four tall towers at the corners of the Taj Mahal?

08. Where did the Emperor Shah Jahan spend the last four years of his life? Why?

09. According to this essay, what color is the Taj Mahal in the morning? in the evening? by moonlight?

CHINESE PAINTING
http://depts.washington.edu/chinaciv/painting/4ptgtech.htm

10. What are four main types of Chinese paintings?

    a) __________ scroll – from two to six feet high and displayed an entire painting at one viewing.

    b) __________ scroll – between nine and fourteen inches in height, but may be as long as twenty-nine feet; only one portion is viewed at a time.

    c) __________ leaves – originating from printing and book binding; they often juxtaposed poetry and painting on opposite pages.

    d) __________ flat oval – often held in one hand.

11. Another format consisted of standing screen paintings. Why did many of these not last?

12. What were the two main types of materials on which paintings were placed? Which surface required more painstaking techniques, building up ink and colors carefully and gradually in layers? Which was more absorbent and was favored for spontaneous effects?

13. What are the colophons on Chinese paintings?

14. Where was the text placed in early Chinese narrative paintings? Beginning around the eleventh century, where was the text placed in relation to the painted image?

15. Is it a good idea to add the text of poetry on to the surface of a painting? Why? Can you think of any examples of Western art that combines text and painting?

16. Inscriptions on Chinese paintings often included appreciative comments of later collectors. What do you think of the idea of later owners adding their views on to the surface of the painting?

17. What is the purpose of the small red seals ("chops") placed on Chinese paintings?

ZEN STORIES
http://www.rider.edu/users/suler/zenstory/zenstory.html
Read the below four very short stories AND then the "people's reactions" printed beneath each story:

– "Books" – "Tea or Iron"

– "Empty Your Cup" – "Working Very Hard"

18. For each story, which of the "people's reactions" was most meaningful to you?

    a) "Books":

    b) "Empty Your Cup":

    c) "Tea or Iron":

    d) "Working Very Hard":

19. Which one story was the most meaningful to you? Why?

20. THE PEOPLES AND CULTURES OF AFRICA

Study Questions:

EARLY AFRICAN KINGDOMS

01. What factors have worked against the formation of a single culture on the African continent?

02. Why is it difficult to generalize about African art and culture?

03. What is meant by "animist beliefs"?

04. What were the names of three important early African Kingdoms?

    – in West Africa (along the upper River Niger)?

    – in west Africa (near present-day Nigeria)?

    – in southern Africa?

05. Around the year C.E. 1000, which African kingdom was probably the world's most important gold producer?

06. What factors contributed to the decline of the ancient kingdom of Ghana?

07. What West African kingdom began to grow in power as the kingdom of Ghana declined?

08. Which African kingdom flourished in the 1300s, 1400s, and early 1500s?

09. What position was held by the "Oba" of Benin?

10. What is the subject of the bronze plaque from Benin shown in Figure 20.1? How can the king be identified? Why are the soldiers shown as small in height?

11. What is the name of the greatest stone ruins yet found in southern Africa? Approximately how many people may have lived there at the height of its power?

12. During the Middle Ages, what new religion was introduced into sub-Saharan Africa?

13. What religion was introduced into Africa during the period of European colonization?

AFRICAN LITERATURE

14. In what respect was early African literature similar to the literature of Homer's *Iliad* and *Odyssey*?

15. Which area of Africa did develop an early written literature? What was the language used?

16. What language influenced Swahili?

17. Who was the most important writer and thinker of twentieth-century Senegal?

18. What did Leopold Senghor mean by "negritude"? In what language did Senghor write? What political position did Senghor hold from 1960 until his retirement in 1980?

19. Who, in 1986, was the first African to receive the Nobel prize for literature?

20. What did Wole Soyinka mean when he said "tigers do not contemplate their 'tigritude' "?

21. Who is generally considered the first African novelist (1875? – 1948)? What is generally considered to be the both the first novel (1906) by an African and the first written in an African language?

22. What is considered to be Thomas Mofolo's most important and successful novel?

23. What is the subject of Mofolo's *Chaka*?

24. Although Mofolo wrote *Chaka* in 1912, why was it not published until 1925?

25. Who is probably the most widely-read and acclaimed African novelist of the twentieth century?

26. What was the title of Chinua Achebe's first book (published in 1948)? What was the source of that title?

27. What is the theme of Achebe's *Things Fall Apart?*

28. Why was Achebe criticized for writing in English? What was Achebe's defense for writing in English?

AFRICAN ART

29. What has been the primary function of traditional African art: aesthetic appreciation or social and religious functions?

30. Why until recently would the idea of a museum or gallery be alien to African art?

31. In traditional African art, how important was the name or identity of the individual creator of art?

32. Who are the two subjects of the Igbo clay figures shown in Figure 20.6? What is significant about the clothing of the male figure? Of the female figure? What conflict is suggested in this work of art?

33. In the house constructed by the Dogon people shown in Figure 30.7, the *Togu na* (men's "house of words"), why do the later posts show more realistic art than the central unpainted post?

34. What was one symbol used by the Yoruba people of western Nigeria to represent the "eternal feminine"?

35. What type of African art was used to transform or to conceal identities?

36. Do African masks usually represent a specific individual or an ideal type?

IMPACT OF AFRICAN CULTURE ON THE WEST

37. What great twentieth-century artist was very influenced by the art of African masks?

38. What part or parts of Picasso's *Les Demoiselles d'Avignon* (Figure 21.1 in the next chapter) show the influence of African art?

39. How does the 1967 *Chicago Picasso* (Figure 20.12) show the influence of African art on Picasso?

40. What important type of American music derives ultimately from the African ancestors of African Americans?

Thought Questions:

A. Which one of the African works of art illustrated in the text did you find most interesting? Why?

B. Why is looking at an African mask in a museum an incomplete experience, perhaps akin to reading a drama rather than seeing an actual performance?

Having a good discussion is like having riches.
– East African proverb (from Kenya)

It takes a village to raise a child.
– West Africa proverb

Define or Identify:

Early African Kingdoms
- Ghana
- Benin
- Zimbabwe

African Literature
- Saiyid Abdullah, "Self Examination"
- Thomas Mofolo, *Traveler of East Africa*, 1906; *Chaka the Zulu*, 1912
- Chinua Achebe, *Things Fall Apart*, 1958
- Wole Soyinka, [*The Lion and the Jewel*, 1963] 1986 Nobel Prize for Literature

African Art
- Bronze showing Oba with his Warriors, Benin, Nigeria, 18th century
- Altar of the Hand, Benin, Nigeria

Impact of African Culture on the West
- Picasso, *Les Demoiselles d'Avignon*, 1907; *Chicago Picasso*, 1967
- Jazz

Other Important Works (Not in the textbook)

Djenne Mosque, Mali, 1300s (rebuilt 1906)
Sankore Mosque, Timbuktu, Mali, early 1400s

African Cinema
- *Hyenas*, Senegal, 1992
- *Clando / Clandestine*, Cameroon, 1993
- *Taafe Fanga / Skirt Power*, Mali, 1997
- *Pieces of Identity*, Congo/Belgium, 1998
- *Hotel Rwanda*, 2004
- *Keïta: The Heritage Of The Griot*, Burkina Faso. 1995

Griot (keeper of the oral tradition "storyteller")

CHAPTER 20 - REVIEW

Begin by writing the title of the chapter you've just studied. Next, without looking at the text or your study guide, use your memory to recall and to list the major sections or topics covered in the chapter. Finally, check your knowledge by taking the short "Self Quiz" below.

A) CHAPTER TITLE:

B) MAJOR SECTIONS OR TOPICS:

C) SELF QUIZ # 20 – IDENTIFY THE:

01. ______________ First great West African kingdom; around C.E. 1000 it was probably the world's most important gold producer.

02. ______________ Most important African kingdom in the 1300s and 1400s.

03. ______________ Greatest kingdom in southern Africa; now the site of the ruins of a large complex of stone buildings.

04. ______________ Religion introduced into Africa during the Middle Ages.

05. ______________ First African novelist, author of *Traveler of the East* (1906) and *Chaka the Zulu* (1912).

06. ______________ Cultural consciousness and literary movement associated with Leopold Senghor.

07. ______________ Most-widely read African novelist of the twentieth-century; author of *Things Fall Apart* (1948).

08. ______________ In 1986, the first African to win the Nobel prize for literature.

09. ______________ Great twentieth-century artist influenced by the art of African masks.

10. ______________ Form of American music derived ultimately from the African ancestors of African Americans.

11. ______________ Keeper of the oral tradition ("storyteller") in many African societies.

20. WEB QUESTS - PEOPLES AND CULTURES OF AFRICA

THE GREAT MOSQUE OF DJENNE
http://www.pbs.org/wonders/Episodes/Epi5/5_wondr2.htm
Click on the small picture in order to see a larger image.

01. In what century was the great Mosque at Djenne built?

02. Why was it built by the ruler Koy Konburo?

03. How old is the building that can be seen today (and that has been named a UNESCO World Heritage site)?

THE SANKORE MOSQUE, TIMBUKTU, MALI
http://www.pbs.org/wonders/Episodes/Epi5/5_wondr6.htm

04. In the early years of what century was the Sankore Mosque built?

05. During the 1500s, what famous center of learning was found within the Sankore Mosque?

06. How did the "University of Timbuktu" ("University of Sankore") differ in organization from medieval European universities?

07. What was the primary focus of instruction of the individual schools located within the Sankore Mosque?

08. What event in the 1590s led to the decline of the university and the deportation of its best scholars?

THE ORAL TRADITION OF THE GRIOTS
http://www.pbs.org/wonders/Episodes/Epi5/5_cultr1.htm

09. What is the name for the keepers of the oral tradition ("storytellers") in many African societies?

10. How have many members of *griot* families become more popular in West Africa and internationally?

AFRICAN ART
http://www.thinker.org/fam/education/publications/guide-african/part-2.html

"How Was This Object Used? What Purpose Did It Serve?"

11. Why was most traditional African art not placed on the walls of a museum to be seen?

12. What are the functions of traditional African art?

13. What is the specific purpose of the Mask with Headdress from the Dan people of Ivory Coast or Liberia (shown on this web page)?

14. Why is this mask out of context in a museum?

CLICK on "Next >>" to advance to the next page.

15. What is the relationship of a "masquerade" to "mask"?

16. In the masking ceremony illustrated, why is the body of the masker completely hidden from view?

17. What important elements of a masquerade are omitted when we only look at a mask in a museum?

CLICK on "Next >>" to advance to the next page.

18. In the Mask of the Maiden Spirit (Igbo people, Nigeria, nineteenth century), why is white pigment used instead of black to inform us this is a spirit?

19. Why have the shapes of a hornbill been placed on the top of the mask?

CLICK on "Next >>" to advance to the next page.

20. In the drum made by the Senufe people who lived in Mali and the Ivory Coast, what animal (believed to be the first animal on earth) was used to represent a messenger between the gods and humans?

CLICK on "Next >>" to advance to the next page.

21. Why were nails and blades inserted into the nineteenth-century figure from the Kongo people that is illustrated on this web page?

CLICK on "Next >>" to advance to the next page.

22. What is the function of the twentieth-century *ibeji* figure from the Yoruba people of Nigeria?

CLICK TWICE on "Next >>" to advance to Slide 11.

23. What is the purpose of the *makpon* from the Dan people of Mali / Ivory Coast?

BRITISH MUSEUM - SAINSBURY AFRICAN GALLERIES
http://www.thebritishmuseum.ac.uk/compass/index.html
[Scroll to the bottom of the page and CLICK on "ALL TOURS," then scroll down to the section on AFRICA, and CLICK on "The African Galleries." CLICK on the specific icons of the below works of art in order to answer the questions. Clicking on the image again will produce a full-frame picture.]

24. BRONZE PLAQUES SHOWING THE OBA OF BENIN WITH ATTENDANTS, Benin City, Nigeria, sixteenth century

    – How many of these plaques can be found in museums in England, Europe and America?

    – What are the subjects of these plaques?

    – In this plaque, why are the two attendants holding up their shields?

    – According to the accounts of early seventeenth-century Dutch explorers, the *oba* or king of Benin covered the piers of his palace courtyard with hundreds of plaques like these. What do you think would be the purpose of such a display?

24. BRONZE HEAD WITH BEADED CROWN AND PLUME, Yoruba, from Ife, Nigeria, c. C.E. twelfth – fourteenth century)

    – Who is portrayed? – Is the appearance of this face realistic?

    – Does the text information about this head suggest that it was usual for other African artists to show their subjects realistically or stylistically?

    – Must art be realistic?

25. IVORY MASK, Edo peoples, probably sixteenth century C.E., from Benin

    – Who does the mask represent?

    – What do the figures at the top represent?

    – In what modern-day country is Benin now located?

26. Sokari Douglas Camp, *BIG MASQUERADE WITH BOAT ON HIS* HEAD, 1995

    – What evidence is there that a blood sacrifice has just taken place?

    – Are masks meant to be in action and used, or displayed in a museum? Is a work designed to be used less of a work of art than objects made specifically to be placed on display?

21. *BETWEEN THE WORLD WARS*

Study Questions:

LITERATURE

01. What impact did the "Great War" of 1914 – 1918 have on the following?

   – the heroic image of war as a "rite of passage"?

   – the Bolshevik Revolution of 1917 in Russia?

   – Fascism and Mussolini's rise to power in Italy?

   – Nazism and Hitler's rise to power in Germany?

   – the optimistic faith in "progress" held in the 19th century by many Europeans?

   – the increase in disillusionment?

02. Who is the author of "The Second Coming"? What does "The Second Coming" suggest about the condition of Western civilization in 1920?

Things fall apart; the centre cannot hold;
Mere anarchy is loosed upon the world. . . .
The best lack all conviction, while the worst
Are full of passionate intensity.

Surely some revelation is at hand;
Surely the Second Coming is at hand....
And what rough beast, its hour come round at last,
Slouches towards Bethlehem to be born?
– "The Second Coming" (1919)

03. What does the title of T.S. Eliot's poem *The Waste Land* (1922) suggest about twentieth-century civilization?

04. Why would T.S. Eliot favor students studying the artistic and religious traditions of the past?

05. What literary form used in Joyce's *Ulysses* was also used in Proust's *Remembrance of Things Past*?

06. Who was the most important Czech author of the 1920s? What is the subject (and mood) of his novel *The Trial* (1925)?

07. What is the meaning of the term "kafkaesque"? What feelings are likely to be aroused by being arrested for a crime that is never named? (How does the emotion in Edvard Munch's *The Scream* (1893) compare with that suggested by the term "kafkaesque"?)

08. According to Virginia Woolf, why have there not been more great women writers?

ART

09. Who were the first two pioneers in Cubist art (between 1908 and 1914)?

10. What was revolutionary about the Cubism of Braque and Picasso (in contrast to the perception of "good art" going back to the Italian Renaissance)?

11. Did Braque and Picasso think painting was essentially a two-dimensional or three-dimensional form of art?

12. Why is Picasso's *Les Demoiselles d'Avignon* (1907) considered a landmark of twentieth-century painting? Which side of the painting shows figures in a more traditional style? Which side contains the more geometric women?

13. What influenced Picasso to repaint the faces in a more "primitive" style?

14. In Braque's *Violin and Palette* (1909 – 1910), how many sides of the violin can be seen? How is this an advantage over traditional "realistic" art?

15. In what way is Picasso's *Daniel-Henry Kahnweiler* (1910) a multi-perspective painting? Can a viewer just look and see the painting, or is the viewer forced to reconstruct the portrait? What is the advantage of such a reconstruction? the disadvantage?

16. What does Picasso's use of rich color and playfulness add to his *Three Musicians* (1921)? Which seems more alive and less intellectual, *Violin and Palette* or *Three Musicians*?

17. What two principal elements of painting are found in Piet Mondrian's *Color Plane in Oval* (c. 1914)? Does this painting tell a story? Does it represent a real object? Do paintings have to tell stories or represent real objects?

18. What Russian-born artist produced works such as *Green Violinist* (1923 – 1924), which included cubism, primitivism, and dreamlike images from his childhood?

19. In the Mexican painter Rufino Tamayo's *Women of Tehuantepec* (1939), where can be seen the influences of Cubism?

20. Which was more important to Kandinsky, color abstractionism or pictorial representation?

21. According to Freud's *The Interpretation of Dreams* (1900), what was the importance of dreams in understanding human beings? Why would Freud's emphasis on the irrational element in man be significant to those who had fought in World War I?

22. Who was the most important Spanish surrealist (1904-1989)? What does his *The Persistence of Memory* (1931) show about his ability to draw images with almost photographic realism? To provide dreamlike quality by violating the laws of physics?

23. In Frida Kahlo's *Self-Portrait Dedicated to Leon Trotsky* (1937), what is interesting about the message on the paper she is holding in her hands?

24. Who was the most famous Belgian surrealist (1898 – 1967)?

25. Why is the title of the Magritte's *Man with a Newspaper* somewhat misleading? Does the painting show the artist's ability to paint images realistically? Is he successful in causing you to wonder and think about what he has done?

MUSIC

26. What form of music was contributed by America to Western civilization? In which American city did it make its first organized appearance?

27. What was W.C. Handy's importance in the development of jazz?

28. What was the name of the first talking motion picture in America?

29. What type of music influenced Kurt Weill and Bertolt Brecht's *Dreigroschenopera (Threepenny Opera)* of 1928, especially in the song "Mack the Knife"?

30. What was the first widely successful American opera (1935)? What type of distinctive American music did it include?

31. With what renaissance in the 1920s and 1930s were African-American writers like Zora Neale Hurston associated?

32. Who was the driving force behind ballet in Paris in the 1920s? What was his contribution to ballet?

ART, PHOTOGRAPHY, FILM

33. What art movement had its origin in 1915 at the Cafe Voltaire in Zurich? What was the meaning of the name applied to this movement?

34. How did Dada feel about the need for good manners, logic, and the past? about the need for spontaneity?

35. What name is given to "sculptures with moving parts"? Which dada artist is associated with this form of art?

36. What name is given to "sculptures constructed from preexisting fabricated materials originally intended for other purposes"?

37. What does Duchamp's version of the "Mona Lisa" suggest about his attitude to art and high culture?

38. What was Picasso's greatest work (1937) of protest?

39. In Picasso's *Guernica*,

    – What event prompted his protest?

    – What are the main colors used in this painting?

    – What image does he use as a symbol for the country of Spain?

    – What image does he use as a "Pietà"?

    – What image shows some hope in the midst of sorrow and evil?

40. What was the importance of the Lumiére Brothers in the history of films?

41. What are two important examples of film as propaganda?

    – 1925: Sergei Eisenstein's ____________________________

    – 1936: Leni Riefenstahl's _____________________________

42. What term is used for Eisenstein's device of conveying an idea or mood by the rapid juxtaposition of different images by the editing of film footage? What is the significance of the Odessa Steps sequence in *Potemkin*?

43. What is the primary subject of Riefenstahl's *Olympia* (1938)? the second subject or theme?

44. What group of people were the subjects of the photographs from the 1930s by Walker Evans published in James Agee's *Let Us Now Praise Famous Men* (1941)?

45. Is photography an art? Why?

46. What name was given to the group of artists in Italy who looked to the future with hope and on the past with contempt? How did they feel about the relationship of industrial civilization and technology to progress?

47. What does Gino Severini's *Armored Train in Action* (1915) seem to say about power, war, and destruction?

48. Which book by Sinclair Lewis in 1922 criticized mindless middle-class materialism?

49. What book by Aldous Huxley in 1932 criticized the totalitarian threat of technology (pleasure machines and pleasure drugs)?

Thought Questions:

A. Do you think the phrase "the waste land" applies today to television today? to abstract art? to modern education? to western civilization?

B. In the 1920s, Ulysses was banned by the U.S. Postal Service as "obscene." Do you think the inability today of the Postal Service to stop people from reading books like *Ulysses* a sign of progress or decay? Why?

C. How does "education" differ from "propaganda"? Do you think Michael Moore's *Fahrenheit 9/11* (2004) was education or propaganda? Why?

D. Which novel do you think is more relevant today, Aldous Huxley's *Brave New World* (whose victims welcome their own enslavement to pleasure) or George Orwell's *1984* (with its vision of a future tyranny of a totalitarian government)? Why?

E. Is it simplistic to identify artists as connected to only one style? Why does this happen?

* *

Nothing is less real than realism. Details are confusing. It is only by selection, be emphasizing, by emphasis, that we get at the real meaning of things.
– Georgia O'Keeffe, 1922

Picasso is not always Picasso; that's why he's Picasso.
– (Statement made in the Picasso Museum, Paris, by a character in Eric Rohmer's film, *Rendezvous in Paris*, 1996)

In spite of everything, I still believe that people are really good at heart.
– Anne Frank, *Diary of Anne Frank*, 1944

Define or Identify:

World War I (1914 – 1918) / World War II (1939 – 1945)
Cubism
Nonrepresentational art
Surrealism
Dada – Marcel Duchamp ("readymades," "mobiles")
Futurism

Significant Works To Recognize and Remember

Freud, *Interpretation of Dreams*, 1900
William Butler Yeats, "The Second Coming," 1919
– "Things fall apart; the centre cannot hold."
T. S. Eliot, *The Waste Land*, 1922
James Joyce, *Ulysses*, 1922
Kafka, *The Trial*, 1926 ("kafkaesque")

Braque, *Violin & Palette*, 1909
Picasso, *Les Demoiselles d'Avignon*, 1907; *Guernica*, 1937
Kandinsky, *Several Circles* [non-representational art], 1926
Mondrian, *Color Planes in Oval*, 1921
Chagall, *Green Violinist*, 1923 – 1924
René Magritte, *Man With A Newspaper*, 1928
Salvador Dali, *The Persistence of Memory*, 1931
Marcel Duchamp, *L.H.O.O.Q.*, 1919
Frida Kahlo, *Self-Portrait Dedicated to Leon Trotsky,* 1937

Eisenstein, *Potemkin*, 1925 (montage)
Riefenstahl, *Triumph of the Will*, 1936; *Olympia,* 1938

Other Important Works (Not in the textbook)

Kandinsky, *The First Abstract Watercolor*, 1912
Chirico, *Melancholy and Mystery of a Street*, 1914
Chagall, *I and the Village,*1911
Delaunay, *Red* Tower 1911, *Disk, First Nonobjective Painting,* 1912
Duchamp, *Fountain,* 1917
Magritte, *This is Not A Pipe*, 1928; *The Human Condition*, 1933
Delvaux, *Pygmalion,*1939; *Evening Train*, 1957
Rouault, *Christ Mocked by Soldiers,* 1932; *The Holy Face,* 1933
Grosz, *Pillars of Society*, 1926
Frida Kahlo, *Two Fridas,* 1939; *Diego in My Thoughts,* 1943
Jacob Lawrence, *The Migration of the Negro,* 1940 – 1941

D.W. Griffith, *Birth of A Nation*, 1915
Welles, *Citizen Kane,* 1939

CHAPTER 21 - REVIEW

Begin by writing the title of the chapter you've just studied. Next, without looking at the text or your study guide, use your memory to recall and to list the major sections or topics covered in the chapter. Finally, check your knowledge by taking the short "Self Quiz" below.

A) CHAPTER TITLE:

B) MAJOR SECTIONS OR TOPICS:

C) SELF QUIZ # 21 – IDENTIFY THE:

01. ______________ Event from 1914 to 1918 which resulted in the disillusionment of Yeats ("The Second Coming") and Eliot (*The Waste Land*).

02. A)____________ First two pioneers of Cubist art (*Les Demoiselles d'Avignon* and *Violin and Palette*).

B)____________

03. ______________ Dada artist (*L.H.O.O.Q.*, 1919) also associated with the creation of "ready-mades" [*Fountain*, 1917].

04. ______________ Pioneer of nonrepresentational art (*Several Circles*, 1926)

05. ______________ Important Czech author (*The Trial*) of the 1920s.

06. ______________ Most important Belgian surrealist (*Man With A Newspaper,* 1928).

07. ______________ Most important Spanish surrealist (*Persistence of Memory*, 1931).

08. ______________ Type of music contributed by America to western civilization (Gershwin's *Porgy and Bess*).

09. ______________ Picasso's great work of protest (1937) against the aerial bombing of a small town in northern Spain.

10. ______________ Term used for Eisenstein's device of conveying an idea or mood by the rapid juxtaposition of different images by the editing of film footage, as in *Potemkin*.

11. ______________ Name of the group of Italian artists who looked to the future with hope and on the past with regret.

21. WEB QUESTS - BETWEEN THE WORLD WARS

MARCEL DUCHAMP'S *FOUNTAIN*
http://collections.sfmoma.org/Obj25853$6083

01. What is the subject of this 1917 "ready-made" (refabricated in 1964 and purchased by the San Francisco Museum of Modern Art)?

02. In one word, what do you think would be Duchamp's answer to the question, "What qualifies as art?"

03. According to a poll in 2004 of five hundred art experts, what was the most influential modern art work of all time, Duchamp's *Fountain,* Picasso's *Les Demoiselles d'Avignon, or* Andy Warhol's *Marilyn Diptych?*
http://news.bbc.co.uk/1/hi/entertainment/arts/4059997.stm

RENÉ MAGRITTE

- THE TREASON OF IMAGES (1928/1929)
http://www.atara.net/magritte/20s/treason.html

04. The text in French tells us that "this is not a pipe." If this is not a pipe, then what is it? (Hint: look at it with the mind of a child.)

- THE HUMAN CONDITION (1933)
http://www.nga.gov/cgi-bin/pinfo?Object=68966+0+none

05. What does *The Human Condition* suggest about the "reality" of painting?

GEORGE GROSZ, *PILLARS OF SOCIETY, 1926*
http://www.art-for-a-change.com/Express/ex10.htm

06. Identify the "pillars of society" from top to bottom (industrialist, clergy, journalist, military, politician):

    - Upper right corner:
    - Upper left corner:
    - Center left:
    - Center right:
    - Lower right:

07. What does the politician seem to have for brains?

08. What dreams are seen in the head of the industrialist?

09. Which figure is wearing the swastika of Hitler and the Nazi Party?

10. What was Hitler's view of the art of George Grosz?

THE PAINTINGS OF FRIDA KAHLO
http://www.fbuch.com/fridaby.htm
View these paintings by Frida Kahlo (and read about her life).

11. Which one of these paintings do you like the most? Why?

12. Which one of these paintings do you like the least? Why?

13. In learning about Frida's life, which web site was better, this one, or the earlier one using Real Audio? Why?

SALVADOR DALÍ
- *SLAVE MARKET WITH THE DISAPPEARING BUST OF VOLTAIRE* (1940)
http://salvadordalimuseum.org/collection/surreal/slave_market.php

14. At what is the woman on the left looking?

15. What image (or two images) replaces the head of Voltaire?

16. What approach to knowledge and understanding does the head of Voltaire represent: Reason or the Irrational?

17. What approach to knowledge and understanding does Dalí use in this painting: Reason or the Irrational?

- THE LAST SUPPER (1955)
http://dali.urvas.lt//forviewing/pic01.jpg
Click in the lower right corner for a very large image.

18. Who is represented at the top of the painting? Why do you think his head is not included?

19. Where (touching Christ) can be seen the Dove / the Holy Spirit?

20. What is unusual about Christ's "physical" body? [Look carefully between his stomach and his left arm.]

- HALLUCINOGENIC TOREADOR (1968 – 1970)
http://salvadordalimuseum.org/collection/classic/the_hallucinogenic_toreador.php

21. What classic statues are found in the center of this work?

22. Where is the face of the toreador? The nose of the toreador is what part of Venus's body? Whose eye becomes the right eye of the toreador?

23. In which corner is there an image of a dying bull? What human image is in the lower right corner of the painting? (Who might this represent as a youngster?)

24. What else did you learn from reading the commentary about this painting?

JACOB LAWRENCE, STORYTELLER - THE MIGRATION OF THE NEGRO
http://www.getty.edu/artsednet/resources/jacoblawrence/2over.htm

25. *Click on each of the numbered paintings listed below, and then write down the narrative text displayed to the right of each work. Click on the image for a larger view or for an even bigger image, click on "largest view".*

    – Panel No. 1:

    – Panel No. 33:

    – Panel No. 45:

    – Panel No. 47:

    – Panel No. 49:

    – Panel No. 59:

    – Panel No. 60:

26. Which image did you like the most? Why?

22. *THE CONTEMPORARY CONTOUR*

Study Questions:

INTRODUCTION

01. According to Freud's *Civilization and Its Discontents* (1929), what price does the individual apparently have to pay to be part of an advanced culture?

02. What philosophy was especially important in Western Europe in the immediate post-war years? Which French writer (1905 – 1980) is most associated with this philosophy?

03. Did Sartre believe in ultimate meaning or an ultimate significance to the universe? Why?

04. What did Sartre mean by "people are condemned to be free"?

05. According to existentialists like Sartre and Albert Camus, who is responsible for finding meaning in life?

PAINTING SINCE 1945

06. In the 1940s and 1950s, what city replaced Paris as the center of modern art?

07. What type of painting was dominant in New York in the post-war period, abstract or representational art?

08. What is the theme or mood of Edward Hopper's *Nighthawks* (1942)?

09. What American painter (1887-1987) is remembered for her paintings of flowers (*Poppy*) that are both representational and abstract?

10. How important is representational art (with recognizable content) to abstract expressionists? What do abstract expressionists use in their paintings to express their inner, subjective, aesthetic experiences?

11. Who was the American leader of the abstract expressionists? What does his *Number 1, 1948* owe to Freud and the surrealists?

12. Why is Jackson Pollock sometimes referred to as "Jack the Dripper"?

13. What traditional elements of painting has Mark Rothko omitted in his murals by expressing emotion by the use of fields of color alone?

14. Why are the works of Jasper Johns and Andy Warhol not seen as examples of abstract expressionism?

15. Which American artist (1930-1987) is most associated with "pop art"? What were some of the subjects of his "pop art"?

16. Why is the term "minimalist" applied to Ellsworth Kelly's *Grey Panels 2* (1974)? Which side is the darker, the left or the right? (Be careful!)

17. What three influences are apparent in Romare Bearden's *The Prevalence of Ritual: Baptism* (1964)?

18. Is Frank Stella's *Shoubeegi / Firebirds* (1978) a painting, a sculpture, or both?

19. Why is Anselm Kiefer's *Innerraum* (1981) considered an example of modern expressionism?

20. In Jaune Quick-to-See Smith's *Indian, Indio, Indigenous* (1992), can you see within her collage the following elements: the masthead of her reservation newspaper (*Char Koosta*), photocopies of George Catlin's drawings of American Indians, part of a U.S. map, pictographs of bear, deer, and a coyote, a painted bust, written declarations, and abstract blocks of paint?

21. What significant color was used for the words "Indian, Indio, Indigenous"? What do you think is the message of this work?

CONTEMPORARY SCULPTURE

22. Why is Alexander Calder's *Big Red* (1959) called a "mobile"?

23. In George Segal's *The Diner* (1966), what mood is created by the use of human figures made from plaster of Paris and set in familiar settings? How does that mood compare with the moods of many of the paintings of Edward Hopper?

24. Which American sculptor (1927 – 1994) is remembered for his works of social comment such as *State Hospital* (1966)?

25. In Henry Moore's *Reclining Figure* (1951), what in the sculpture represents the forces of life? of death? of sexuality?

26. Why is "hyperrealistic" a good term to describe such works of Duane Hanson as *The Dockman* (1979)?

27. In Rachel Whiteread's *Memorial to the Victims of the Holocaust* at Judenplatz in Vienna (2000), what is the significance of showing the library inside-out, with shelves of closed books facing inwards so that not even their titles can be seen?

ARCHITECTURE

28. Who was the most influential American architect of the twentieth century? Who was his teacher?

29. Which one built in the 1890s the first skyscraper in the United States?

30. What did Louis Sullivan mean by "form follows function"?

31. What did Wright mean by "organic architecture"?

32. What advantage to the museumgoer is there in Frank Lloyd Wright's design for the Guggenheim Museum in New York (1957 – 1959)?

33. What modern principle is associated with the German Bauhaus school of design?

34. Why did the architects Walter Gropius and Miës van der Rohe migrate to the United States in the 1930s?

35. How does modern architecture, such as the Seagram Building (designed by Miës van der Rohe and Philip Johnson), represent the belief that "less is more"?

36. What is striking about the exterior of the Georges Pompidou National Center for Art and Culture (1977) in Paris? Is this building characterized by the austerity and simplicity of the Bauhaus school? [The Pompidou Center has become the #2 tourist attraction in France. Disneyland Paris is #1 and the Louvre is #5.]

37. Why would the term "exo-skeletal architecture" be appropriate in describing the Pompidou Center?

38. How is "post-modern architecture" different from the modern architecture inspired by the Bauhaus school?

FILM, LITERATURE AND MUSIC

39. What questions are explored by the Swedish filmmaker Ingmar Bergman (1918 –) in his films *such as Wild Strawberries* (1956) [or *The Seventh Seal* (1957) or *Fanny and Alexander* (1983)]?

40. What appears to be the meaning of Samuel Beckett's *Waiting for Godot* (1952)?

41. What meaning to life was found by Elie Wiesel (*Night*, 1960) after surviving life in concentration/ extermination camps as a child?

42. What does Arthur Miller's *Death of A Salesman* (1949) suggest about the meaning of life (and the fate of the "American Dream")?

43. What are the subjects of Richard Wright's *Native Son* (1940) and Ralph Ellison's *Invisible Man* (1952)?

44. What is aleatory music? How is it similar to the works of Jackson Pollock?

45. What term is applied to the music of Steve Reich, which builds lengthy pieces out of multiple repetition of simple chords and rhythms?

46. What type of non-western music has influenced the work of the minimalist composer Philip Glass?

47. What is meant by the term "global culture"? What form of art best supports the thesis of "global culture"?

Thought Questions:

A. How does technology contribute to standardization? to individualism?

B. Why does no one style dominate art today?

C. Is America characterized more by "pluralism" or by a "common culture"?

D. How is the debate over a "global culture" vs. "pluralism" reflected in the debates over which books and works of art should be required in core humanities courses?

E. Is life absurd and without meaning? Where can one find "meaning" in today's world? [You have the rest of your life to work on this.]

My whole life has been dedicated to the idea that people are more alike than they are different, that we all want the same things.

– Maya Angelou

If there's someone you love but haven't said so in a while, say it now. Always, always, say it now.

– Mike Royko, *Newsweek*, May 12, 1997, p. 60.
(Written in the *Chicago Daily News* in 1979,
after the death of his wife.)

Define or Identify:

"Global Culture"
Existentialism: Jean-Paul Sartre
Abstract Expressionism: Jackson Pollock
Color Field Painting: Mark Rothko
Pop Art: Andy Warhol
Minimalism (Ellsworth Kelly, *Grey Panels 2*)
Louis Sullivan, "form follows function"
Frank Lloyd Wright, organic architecture
Alexander Calder (mobiles)
Bauhaus School
Miës van der Rohe ["less is more"]
Post-modern architecture

Significant Works To Recognize and Remember

Freud, *Civilization and Its Discontents*, 1929
George Orwell, *Animal Farm*, 1945; *1984*, 1949
Samuel Beckett, *Waiting for Godot*, 1952
Arthur Miller, *Death of A Salesman*, 1949
Elie Wiesel, *Night*, 1960
Ralph Ellison, *Invisible Man*, 1952

Edward Hopper, *Nighthawks*, 1942
Georgia O'Keeffe, *Poppy*, 1927
Romare Bearden, *The Prevalence of Ritual: Baptism*, 1964
Jackson Pollock, *Number 1, 1948*
Mark Rothko, *Rothko Chapel Murals*, Rice University, 1971
Frank Stella, *Shoubeegi / Indian Birds*, 1978
Jaune Quick-to-See Smith, *Indian, Indio, Indigenous,* 1992

Alexander Calder, *Big Red*, 1959
Henry Moore, *Reclining Figure*, 1951
George Segal, *The Diner*, 1966
Duane Hanson, *The Dockman*, 1979

Frank Lloyd Wright, Guggenheim Museum, NYC, 1957 – 1960
Miës van der Rohe & Philip Johnson, Seagram Building, NYC, 1958
Renzo Piano and Richard Rogers, Pompidou Centre, Paris, 1977
I.M. Pei, National Gallery East Wing, Washington D.C., c. 1992
Maya Ying Lin, *Vietnam Veterans Memorial*, Washington D.C.,1983
Herzog and De Meuron, Tate Modern, London, 2000
Jaume Plensa, Crown Fountain, Millennium Park, Chicago, 2004

Other Important Works (Not in the textbook)

Edward Hopper, *Hotel Room,* 1931; *New York Movie*, 1939
Paul Delvaux, *Pygmalion*, 1939; *Evening Train*, 1957
Francis Bacon, *Study After Velázquez*, 1953
Salvador Dali, *The Last Supper*, 1955; *Hallucinogenic Toreador*, 1968-70
Jasper Johns, *Three Flags*, 1958; *White Flag*, 1955
Andy Warhol, *Marilyn Diptych*, 1962; *Ten Lizzes*, 1963
George Tooker, *Government Bureau*, 1956; *Lunch*, 1964
Roy Lichtenstein, *Masterpiece!,"* 1962; *Drowning Girl,* 1963; *WHAAMM!,* 1963
Faith Ringgold, *American People Series #19: Us Postage Commemorating The Advent Of Black Power,* 1967; *Freedom of Speech*, 1990
David Hockney, *Mr and Mrs Clark and Percy*, 1971; *Pear Blossom Highway*, 1986
Judy Chicago, *The Dinner Party*, 1973-79
Mark Tansey, *The Innocent Eye Test*, 1981; *Triumph Over Mastery II,* 1987
Bill Viola: *Quintet Of The Astonished*, 2000

Alberto Giacometti, *Man Pointing,*1947; *City Square / La Place*, 1948
Edward Kienholz, *Back Seat Dodge '38*, 1964
Claes Oldenburg, *Clothespin*, 1976

Johnson & Burgee, A T & T Building, New York, 1980
I.M. Pei, Glass Pyramid Entrance, Louvre, Paris, 1989
Frank Gehry, Guggenheim Museum, Bilbao, Spain, 1997
Santiago Calatrava, Milwaukee Art Museum, 2003
Norman Foster, Swiss Re Headquarters, London, 2004

Gabriel García Márquez, *One Hundred Years of Solitude*, 1967
Kurt Vonnegut, Jr., *Slaughterhouse-Five,*1969
Nazim Hikmet, *Human Landscapes: An Epic Novel in Verse*, 1982
Art Spiegleman, *Maus: A Survivor's Tale*, 1986; *Maus II*, 1991
Marjane Satrapi, *Persepolis: The Story of a Childhood,* 2003

J.B. Priestley, *An Inspector Calls,* 1945
Joan Littlewood, *Oh What A Lovely War*, 1963
Tom Stoppard, *Rosencrantz and Guildenstern Are Dead*, 1967;
Caryl Churchill, *Cloud Nine*, 1979
David Mamet, *Glengarry Glen Ross*, 1984
August Wilson, *Fences*, 1987; *Gem of the Ocean*, 2004

Aesthetics is for the artist as ornithology is for the birds.
– Barnett Newman (Abstract Expressionist)

CHAPTER 22 - REVIEW

Begin by writing the title of the chapter you've just studied. Next, without looking at the text or your study guide, use your memory to recall and to list the major sections or topics covered in the chapter. Finally, check your knowledge by taking the short "Self Quiz" below.

A) CHAPTER TITLE:

B) MAJOR SECTIONS OR TOPICS:

C) SELF QUIZ # 22 – IDENTIFY THE:

01. ______________ Philosophy associated with Jean Paul Sartre ("People are condemned to be free") and Albert Camus.

02. ______________ City that in the 1940s replaced Paris as the center of modern art.

03. ______________ "Exo-skeletal" building and Paris modern art center.

04. ______________ American painter of flowers and desert scenes.

05. ______________ American painter of urban loneliness (*Nighthawks*)

06. ______________ Art style associated with Jackson Pollock (*Number 1, 1948*).

07. ______________ Artist remembered for painting large fields of color forms such as the panels for a chapel at Rice University, Texas.

08. ______________ Type of art associated with Andy Warhol.

09. ______________ Artist known for "mobiles" like *Big Red* (1959)

10. ______________ Most influential American architect of the twentieth century (Guggenheim Museum, New York City)

11. ______________ Type of architecture today which uses decoration for the sake of beauty and rejects Bauhaus simplicity ("less is a bore").

22. WEB QUESTS - CONTEMPORARY CONTOUR

UNDERSTANDING ABSTRACT ART
http://www.harley.com/art/abstract-art/index.html

01. What are the two broad types of paintings indicated in the fourth paragraph?

02. What are the two types of abstract paintings?

- Which type is represented by art such as Monet's *Water Lilies [The Clouds] (1903)*?

- Which type is represented by Kandinsky's *Improvisation 7* (1910) and Jackson Pollock's *Number 1, 1950* [Lavender Mist] (1950)?

03. According to this essay, which type of art has the "ability to bypass our consciousness and stir our inner feelings"?

04. What was the reaction of the author of this essay upon Jackson Pollock's *Lavender Mist* in the National Gallery of Art, Washington D.C.?

05. Of the seventeen paintings displayed on this web page, which one was the most successful in creating a feeling of emotion within you?

GEORGIA O'KEEFFE
http://www.michelangelo.com/okeeffe/index-ns.html
CLICK on the flower icon at the top of the page, then CLICK the icons in the lower-left corner for information and to a larger image.

06. a. What are the titles of these works by Georgia O'Keeffe?
   – Upper-left corner – 1927:
   – Upper-right corner – c. 1923:
   – Lower-left corner – 1926:

   b. Why did O'Keeffe paint big flowers? *(Read the quotation beneath the large image of "Poppy".)*

   c. What statement of O'Keeffe is found beneath large image of *Red Canna?*

   d. Which one of these pictures do you like the most? WHY?

ANDY WARHOL
- MARILYN MONROE
http://puffin.creighton.edu/museums/archive/7_abarnett/page2.htm

07. Why would Andy Warhol be able to sympathize with Marilyn Monroe's interest in being taken seriously as an artist?

- **ELVIS**

http://puffin.creighton.edu/museums/archive/7_abarnett/elvis.htm

08. What did Andy Warhol have in common with Marilyn Monroe and Elvis Presley?

- **DOLLAR BILL**

http://puffin.creighton.edu/museums/archive/7_abarnett/dollar.htm

09. What does the painting suggest about the relationship of the world of art to the commercial marketplace?

JUDY CHICAGO: *THE DINNER PARTY* (1974 – 1979)
http://www.judychicago.com/judychicago.php?p=dinnerparty1
CLICK on "Next" or on the appropriate number at the bottom of the page to view the below frames:

10. Frame 1: What is the subject of the thirty-nine place settings?

11. Frame 2: How many names are found on the porcelain floor between the three sides of the table?

12. Frame 4: When Judy Chicago studied as an undergraduate at UCLA in the 1960s, how many women appeared in the standard art history college textbook by H.W. Jansen.

13. Frame 6: Who is the subject of this place setting? Why was her achievement? (See Chapter 11 in the textbook.)

14. Frame 10: What three women are honored by the place settings shown in this frame?

15. Do you consider *The Dinner Party* to be a work of art that should be on exhibit in a museum? Why or why not?

MAYA LIN – THE VIETNAM VETERANS MEMORIAL, WASHINGTON, D.C. (1988)
http://www.loc.gov/exhibits/treasures/trm022.html
Lin initially submitted the design for the D.C. memorial for an assignment when she was a twenty-one year-old-student in a class at Yale University's School of Architecture. She received a B.

16. How did Maya Lin envision the Vietnam Veterans Memorial?

17. What was her hope in placing the names on the memorial?

Great Buildings Online
http://www.greatbuildings.com/buildings/Vietnam_Veterans_Memorial.html

18. To what Monument and to what Memorial do its walls point?

19. Are the names inscribed alphabetically or chronologically? Why?

20. Do you think the Memorial should be seen as architecture or as landscape design? Why?

21. What image is reflected in the polished black walls of the Vietnam Veterans Memorial? [*See photo close-up.]*

Civil Rights Memorial, Birmingham, Alabama
http://www.splcenter.org/crm/memorial.jsp

22. How was Maya Lin's design influenced by the words "until justice rolls down like waters and righteousness like a mighty stream" (words used by Dr. Martin Luther King in his "I Have a Dream" speech and at the start of the bus boycott in Montgomery eight years earlier)?

23. *CLICK on "Launch" (just to the right of the photograph) to see ten photographs about the memorial.* What are people actually touching on the memorial?

DAVID HOCKNEY, *PEARBLOSSOM HWY*, 11-18th April 1986, #1 and **#2**
http://www.getty.edu/art/collections/objects/o113244.html

24. Why does this view of the highway appear to look odd? (*Click on "Enlarge" for a clearer view.)*

25. What does Hockney mean when he said he said this work was "a panoramic assault on Renaissance one-point perspective"?

http://www.getty.edu/art/collections/objects/o112574.html

26. Why does the road appear differently on the right-side of the picture as compared with the left side?

VISIT: MARK TANSEY (1949 -)
- THE INNOCENT EYE TEST, 1981
http://www.eng.umu.se/litgrad/innocent.htm

27. What do you think is the meaning of this painting? How much professional training does a person need to judge whether a painting is good or bad?

- TRIUMPH OVER MASTERY, 1987
http://www.uncommon-sense.net/interests/art/tansey/triumph.jpg

28. How much artistic skill is being used by the man on the ladder?

29. What is the title of the painting originally on the wall and now being completely covered over? (Hint: review Chapter 13.)

30. What is happening to the man's shadow on the wall being painted?

BILL VIOLA: *QUINTET OF THE ASTONISHED*, 2000
http://www.getty.edu/art/exhibitions/viola/quintet.html
CLICK on the top icon "Influences from Past Art."

31. What is the title of the Bosch paintings which influenced Bill Viola? Who is in the center of the painting and at whom is he looking?

CLICK on the other icon labeled "Influences from Past Art." When Bill Viola begins speaking, CLICK on "Zoom" to see a larger image of the painting.

32. According to Bill Viola's comments on the Audio Clip about Mantegna's *Adoration of the Magi,* at what are four of the five adults looking? Do they seem to be relating to each other despite their shared intense emotional experience?

To see several minutes from the Bill Viola's "Quintet of the Astonished," CLICK on "Play Video Excerpt." Then choose your Internet connection speed. (The QuickTime plug-in is required to view this video. If necessary, click the QuickTime logo to get the free download.)

33. Does the use of silence and slow motion encouraged thought? How much on television uses silence slow motion to encourage thought?

FAITH RINGGOLD: *THE AMERICAN PEOPLE SERIES #19: U.S. POSTAGE COMMEMORATING THE ADVENT OF BLACK POWER,* 1967
http://www.faithringgold.com/ringgold/d73.htm

34. How many faces are depicted? How many of the faces are white? How many are black?

35. What two words are shown in black ink?

36. What two words are shown in white ink? (Look carefully. It may be helpful to view the stamp from an angle with the left side at the bottom.)

LEARNING TO THINK LIKE AN ARTIST
http://www.arts.ufl.edu/art/rt_room/%40rtrageous/think_like_an_artist.html

"What Does it Mean to Think Like An Artist" contains a list of characteristics suggested by Dr. Craig Roland, Associate Professor, University of Florida Department of Art.

37. Which five characteristics do you think are most important? Explain the reasons for your choices.

 a) ______________________________

 b) ______________________________

 c) ______________________________

 d) ______________________________

 e) ______________________________

38. Place a circle around those characteristics which you believe you have?

Everything is interesting if you look at it deeply enough.
— Richard Feynman (1965 Nobel Prize winner, quantum electrodynamics)

END OF SECTION REVIEW OF NINETEENTH & TWENTIETH CENTURIES

Match the descriptions below with the correct answers:

_____	1.	Balzac	A.	19th-century art of emotion & Nature
_____	2.	Beckett	B.	German musical romanticist (*Pathétique*)
_____	3.	Beethoven	C.	Greatest Italian composer of 1800s (*Aida*)
_____	4.	*Belle Époque*	D.	German composer (*Ring of the Niebelung*)
_____	5.	Bergman	E.	Spanish romantic artist (*The 3rd of May*)
_____	6.	Calder	F.	French romantic artist (*Raft of the Medusa*)
_____	7.	Cassatt	G.	German romantic artist (*Cloister Graveyard*)
_____	8.	Cézanne	H.	English "pre-impressionist" (*Slave Ship*)
_____	9.	Cubism	I	Art style of Gustave Courbet
_____	10.	Dada	J.	German literary genius (*Faust*)
_____	11.	Dali	K.	French Realist Novelist (*Human Comedy*)
_____	12.	Dickens	L.	English Realist novelist (*Oliver Twist*)
_____	13.	Dostoevsky	M.	American lover of nature & solitude
_____	14.	Eisenstein	N.	"Beautiful Age" from 1890-1914
_____	15.	Existentialism	O.	French artist who influenced Monet, etc
_____	16.	Fauvism	P.	Father of Impressionism (*Impression:Sunrise*).
_____	17.	Freud	Q.	Impressions of happy people in Paris
_____	18.	Friedrich	R.	Most important American impressionist
_____	19.	Gauguin	S.	Dots of pure color, by Seurat
_____	20.	Géricault	T.	Post-impressionist painter of Tahitians
_____	21.	Goethe	U.	Dutch Post-Impressionist (*Starry Night*)
_____	22.	Goya	V.	Artist seeking geometric order
_____	23.	*Guernica*	W.	Greatest sculptor of the 1800s (*The Kiss*)
_____	24.	Great War	X.	Russian novelist (*Crime & Punishment*)
_____	25.	Hopper	Y.	Norwegian Realist playwright
_____	26.	Ibsen	Z.	Norwegian Expressionist artist (*TheScream*)
_____	27.	Kafka	AA.	Pioneer of non-representational art
_____	28.	Kandinsky	BB.	Painting by "wild beasts" such as Matisse
_____	29.	Magritte	CC.	Multi-dimensional art of Braque & Picasso
_____	30.	Manet	DD.	Picasso's greatest protest painting
_____	31.	Monet	EE.	Protest art of Marcel Duchamp, and others
_____	32.	Munch	FF.	Stream-of-consciousness writer
_____	33.	New York City	GG.	Disillusioning event from 1914 to 1918
_____	34.	O'Keeffe	HH.	"Things fall apart" ("The Second Coming")
_____	35.	Paris	II.	Czech "kafkaesque" author (*The Trial*)
_____	36.	Pointillism	JJ.	Inventor of montage (*Potemkin*)
_____	37.	Pollock	KK.	Most important Spanish surrealist
_____	38.	Proust	LL.	Belgian Surrealist (*Man With a Newspaper*)
_____	39.	Realism	MM.	Philosophy of Jean Paul Sartre
_____	40.	Renoir	NN.	Psychotherapist: Humans are irrational
_____	41.	Rodin	OO.	American painter of flowers and desert scenes
_____	42.	Romanticism	PP.	American painter of urban loneliness
_____	43.	Thoreau	QQ.	Capital city of art in the 1920s
_____	44.	Turner	RR.	Capital city of art in the 1950s
_____	45.	Van Gogh	SS.	American Abstract Expressionist
_____	46.	Verdi	TT.	American pop artist
_____	47.	Wagner	UU.	Artist of "mobiles" (*Big Red*)
_____	48.	Warhol	VV.	Form follows Function in architecture
_____	49.	Wright, Frank L.	WW.	Theater of the Absurd; *Waiting for Godot*
_____	50.	Yeats	XX.	Swedish film director (*Wild Strawberries*)

REVIEW IV- B – GEOGRAPHY: NINETEENTH & TWENTIETH CENTURY EUROPE

YOUR ASSIGNMENT:

A) Use the maps in your textbook to identify the locations marked on the map below.

B) Select from the below list the name of an artist, author or filmmaker to match the place you've identified.

Eisenstein	Magritte	Munch	Severini
Goya	Mondrian	Renoir	Turner

C) Provide the title of a work of art by that artist.

A)	Location on Map:	B) Artist:		C) Work of Art:
1. _____	MADRID	____________________	=	____________________
2. _____	PARIS	____________________	=	____________________
3. _____	LONDON	____________________	=	____________________
4. _____	OSLO	____________________	=	____________________
5. _____	BRUSSELS+	____________________	=	____________________
6. _____	ROME	____________________	=	____________________
7. _____	MOSCOW	____________________	=	____________________
8. _____	AMSTERDAM	____________________	=	____________________

+NOT ON A MAP IN THE TEXTBOOK

REVIEW – ROMANTICISM TO SURREALISM – QUOTATIONS

Match the artists below with their quotations (the quotations are not in the textbook; try to figure out who would have said these statements):

CÉZANNE	GAUGUIN	KANDINSKY	MUNCH	RODIN
COURBET	DALÍ	MAGRITTE	RENOIR	VAN GOGH

01. ___________ "I have never seen an angel. Show me an angel and I will paint one. Everything that does not appear on the retina is outside the domain of painting."

02. ___________ "A picture must be an amiable thing, joyous and pretty."

03. ___________ "Civilization is what you are suffering from; to me barbarism is a rejuvenation."

04. ___________ "Vast stretches of wheat under troubled skies . . . . I did not need to go out of my way to express sadness and the extreme of loneliness."

05. ___________ "Reproduce nature in terms of the cylinder & the sphere and the cone."

06. ___________ "I sought in 'Balzac' . . . to render in sculpture what was not photographic."

07. ___________ "One evening I was walking along a path, the city was on one side and the fjord below. I felt tired and ill. I stopped and looked over the fjord—the sun was setting, and the clouds turning blood red. I sensed a scream through nature; it seemed to me that I heard the scream."

08. ___________ "I was suddenly confronted by a picture of indescribable and incandescent loveliness. Bewildered I stopped, staring at it. The painting lacked all subject, depicted no identifiable object and was entirely composed of bright color patches. Finally I approached closer and, only then, recognized it for what it was—my own painting, standing on its side on the easel."

09. ___________ "Ceci n'est pas une pipe"/ "This is not a pipe."

10. ___________ "The only difference between a madman and myself is that I am not mad."

END OF SECTION REVIEW – NINETEENTH CENTURY ART

Identify the artists of the paintings listed below:

ROMANTICISM

01. ____________________ *Third of May, 1808; Sleep of Reason Produces Monsters*
02. ____________________ *Raft of the Medusa*
03. ____________________ *Massacre at Chios; Death of Sardanapalus*
04 ____________________ *Cloister Graveyard in the Snow;Wanderer Above the Mist*
05. ____________________ *Newton; Nebuchadnezzar*
06. ____________________ *Salisbury Cathedral; Flatford Mill*
07.____________________ *Slave Ship; Rain, Steam, Speed; The Fighting Téméraire*

REALISM

08. ____________________ *The Studio; Burial at Ornans*
09. ____________________ *The Legislative Belly; Third-Class Carriage*
10. ____________________ *Eagle Head, Manchester, Mass; Snap the Whip*
11. ____________________ *The Banjo Lesson*

IMPRESSIONISM

12._ ____________________ *Luncheon on the Grass; Olympia; Bar at Folies Bergere*
13. ____________________ *Impression: Sunrise; Rouen Cathedral; Water Lilies*
14. ____________________ *At the Moulin de la Galette; The Boating Party*
15. ____________________ *The Dance Rehearsal; Fourteen-Year Old Ballet Dancer*
16. ____________________ *View of Paris from the Trocadero; The Cradle*
17. ____________________ *Mother and Child; Children Playing on the Beach*

POST-IMPRESSIONISM

18. ____________________ *Sunday Afternoon on La Grande Jatte*
19. ____________________ *Mont Sainte-Victoire*
20. ____________________ *Ia Orana Maria (We Hail Thee Mary); Nevermore*
21. ____________________ *Starry Night; Night Cafe; Self Portraits; Dr. Gachet*
22. ____________________ *The Kiss* (1886); *The Thinker; Monument to Balzac*

EARLY EXPRESSIONISM

23. ____________________ *The Scream*

ART NOUVEAU

24. ____________________ *The Kiss* (1907)
25. ____________________ *Jack-in-the-Pulpit Vase; Tiffany Lamps*

Blake	Friedrich	Monet	Turner
Cassat	Gauguin	Morisot	Seurat
Cézanne	Géricault	Munch	Van Gogh
Constable	Goya	Renoir	
Courbet	Homer		
Daumier		Rodin	
Degas	Klimt	Tanner	
Delacroix	Manet	Tiffany	

END OF SECTION REVIEW – TWENTIETH CENTURY ART

Identify the artists of the paintings listed below:

FAUVISM AND CUBISM

01. ____________________ *Joy of Life*; *The Dance*; *Red Studio; Blue Nude, The Snail*
02. ____________________ *Violin and Palette; Man with a Guitar*
03. ____________________ *Demoiselles D'Avignon; The Three Musicians; Guernica*

EARLY ABSTRACT AND NON-REPRESENTATIONAL

04. ____________________ *Color Planes in Oval; Composition in Red, Yellow, Blue*
05. ____________________ *First Abstract Water Color; Several Circles*
06. ____________________ *The Kiss; Sleeping Muse; Bird; Bird in Space (Flight)*
07. ____________________ *Fish; Big Red (Mobiles)*

DADAISM

08. ____________________ *Fountain; Bicycle Wheel; L.H.O.O.Q.*

DREAMLIKE AND SURREALISM

09. ____________________ *Green Violinist; I and the Village*
10. ____________________ *Man with a Newspaper; The False Mirror; This is Not a Pipe*
11. ____________________ *Persistence of Memory; Hallucinogenic Toreador; Last Supper*

REPRESENTATIONAL ART: 1920-1945

12. ____________________ *Self Portrait Dedicated to Leon Trotsky; Diego on My Mind*
13. ____________________ *Hotel Room; New York Movie; Nighthawks*
14. ____________________ *Poppy*; *Jack-in-the-Pulpit II - VI*
15. ____________________ *Migration of the Negro* Series

ABSTRACT EXPRESSIONISM: ACTION PAINTING / COLOR FIELD PAINTING

16. ____________________ *Number 1, 1948; Lavender Mist (Number 1, 1950)*
17. ____________________ *Black on Maroon* (Color Field paintings)

POP ART AND CONTEMPORARY ART

18. ____________________ *Flag; Three Flags; White Flag*
19. ____________________ *Brillo; Ten Lizzes; Marilyn Diptych; Mick Jagger*
20. ____________________ *Viet-Nam Memorial*
21. ____________________ *The Dinner Party*
22. ____________________ *Memorial to the Victims of the Holocaust*, Vienna (2000)

ARCHITECTURE

23. ____________________ Guggenheim Museum (1959)
24. ____________________ East Wing, National Gallery, D.C.; Glass Pyramid, Louvre, Paris
25. ____________________ American Center, Paris; Guggenheim Museum, Bilbao, Spain

Braque
Brancusi
Calder
Chagall
Chicago
Dalí
Duchamp
Gehry
Hopper
Johns
Kahlo
Kandinsky
Lawrence
Lin
Magritte
Matisse
Mondrian
O'Keeffe
Pei
Picasso
Pollock
Rothko
Warhol
Whiteread
Wright

FINAL REVIEW I -A – ARTISTS

Identify the artists described below (using the list at the bottom of the page).

01. ____________________ Early Renaissance artist who rediscovered the skill of realistic perspective

02. ____________________ Florentine painter of Renaissance beauties

03. ____________________ Multi-talented "renaissance man"

04. ____________________ Greatest Renaissance sculptor

05. ____________________ Pioneered oil paintings; *Arnolfini Marriage*

06. ____________________ Northern Renaissance woodcut genius

07. ____________________ Peasant life scenes in Flanders

08. ____________________ Elongated, spiritual bodies

09. ____________________ Greatest Spanish Baroque artist

10. ____________________ Greatest Dutch painter, *Night Watch*

11. ____________________ First important French rococo painter

12. ____________________ Most important French neo-classical painter

13. ____________________ Quiet scenes, ordinary Dutch life

14. ____________________ Spanish Romantic painter; dark scenes of life

15. ____________________ French "Pre-impressionist"; *Luncheon on the Grass*

16. ____________________ Father of Impressionism; *Impression: Sunrise*

17. ____________________ Impressionist: beautiful women & happy scenes

18. ____________________ Most important American impressionist

19. ____________________ Dutch Impressionist/Expressionist

20. ____________________ Post-Impressionist: native scenes

21. ____________________ Post-Impressionist: Geometric order

22. ____________________ Greatest nineteenth-century sculptor; *The Kiss*

23. ____________________ Greatest painter of twentieth century

BOTTICELLI	DAVID	GIOTTO	MICHELANGELO	RENOIR	VELÁZQUEZ
BRUEGEL	DURER	GOYA	MONET	RODIN	VERMEER
CASSATT	EL GRECO	LEONARDO	PICASSO	VAN EYCK	WATTEAU
CÉZANNE	GAUGUIN	MANET	REMBRANDT	VAN GOGH	

FINAL REVIEW I -B – ARTISTS

Match the artists listed in left column with the correct description in the right column:

A) BOTTICELLI (d. 1510)	____	Belgian Surrealist
B) BRUEGEL (d. 1569)	____	Dutch Expressionist
C) CASSATT (d. 1926)	____	Elongated, spiritual bodies
D) CÉZANNE (d. 1906)	____	Father of Impressionism
E) DALÍ (d. 1989)	____	First important Rococo Painter
F) DAVID (d. 1825)	____	French Neo-classical painter
G) DEGAS (d. 1917)	____	Geometric order, Post-Impressionist
H) DÜRER (d. 1528)	____	Greatest Dutch painter
I) EL GRECO (d. 1614)	____	Greatest 19th-century sculptor
J) GAUGUIN (d. 1903)	____	Greatest painter of 20th century
K) GIOTTO (d. 1337)	____	Greatest Renaissance sculptor
L) GOYA (d. 1828)	____	Greatest Venetian painter
M) LEONARDO (d. 1519)	____	Impressions of beautiful women
N) MAGRITTE (d. 1967)	____	Impressions of ballet
O) MANET (d. 1883)	____	Influenced many Impressionists
P) MICHELANGELO (d. 1564)	____	Important U.S. Impressionist
Q) MONET (d. 1926)	____	Native scenes, bright colors
R) PICASSO (d. 1973)	____	Northern Renaissance woodcuts
S) REMBRANDT (d. 1669)	____	Peasant life scenes
T) RENOIR (d. 1919)	____	Pioneered oil paintings
U) RODIN (d. 1917)	____	Quiet scenes of Dutch life
V) TITIAN (d. 1576)	____	Rediscovered perspective
W) VAN EYCK (d. 1441)	____	Renaissance female beauties
X) VAN GOGH (d. 1890)	____	Spanish Romantic painter
Y) VERMEER (d. 1675)	____	Spanish Surrealist
Z) WATTEAU (d. 1721)	____	The "Renaissance man"

FINAL REVIEW I -C – 25 ARTISTS AND THEIR PAINTINGS

Name the artist and the title of the paintings described below:

01. Two people from Italy are married in Bruges, while the artist, reflected in a round mirror, looks on as a witness.

02. It's spring, and in an Italian orange grove are found the god Mercury, three dancing graces, Cupid flying above ready to let loose his arrow of love, and the wind god (Zephyr) pursuing a nymph who becomes the goddess Flora.

03. Jesus, seated at a table with his disciples, announces that one of them will betray him.

04. The greatest teachers and philosophers of ancient Greece mingle together on a wall in the Office of Signatures in the Vatican.

05. God is about to give the spark of life to a not quite awakened Adam.

06. A German knight, with calm determination, continues on his path despite the appearance of Death and the Devil.

07. In a triptych, between scenes of Eden on the left and the Last Judgment on the right, hundreds of naked figures frantically seek pleasure.

08. The "bride to be" beams happily, the prospective groom has another drink, a monk talks with the wealthy landlord, and a child continues to feed his mouth.

09. Sitting at a card table with four others, a player receives his calling, but responds by pointing at himself and apparently asking, "Me?"

10. "What lives well, lives quietly." A young woman reads a letter with the help of light coming from the window on her left. On the wall behind her hangs a map.

11. The most famous self portrait (at age 63) by a Dutch Baroque artist.

12. After a day of pleasure, aristocratic ladies and gentlemen leave the island birthplace of Venus.

13. In England, a marriage arranged for a title or wealth leads to disaster for all.

14. Three brothers swear an oath to their father to defend Rome, even at the cost of their lives.

15. The new leader, mounted on a white horse, proceeds past stones marked with the names of Charlemagne and Hannibal.

16. Instead of finding Liberty, Equality, Fraternity, citizens of Madrid are shot down by a firing squad at night.

17. It's Paris in 1863 and two couples are having a picnic on the grass, but one woman has forgotten to wear any clothing.

18. Young men and women enjoy the pleasures of urban life in a popular Parisian restaurant and dance hall.

19. The ugliness and harshness of life in a cafe at night "where one can ruin oneself, go mad, or commit a crime."

20. A mountain in southern France painted to show the underlying order in nature, that is, rectangles, spheres, and cones.

21. A person crossing a bridge, with two figures on the far end of the bridge and a fjord in the background, holds two hands to the head in anguish at hearing the scream in nature.

22. Five highly angular women are at work in their house at Avignon Street in Barcelona; they are staring at the viewer trying to catch his attention.

23. A man plays his violin while standing on the roofs of two houses in his native Russia; a man flying above his head adds to the dream-like atmosphere.

24. Drooping watches hang from a tree and over a ledge while ants wander over the closed face of a pocket watch.

25. Late at night, three people sit at a café counter; they appear lonely and isolated.

FINAL REVIEW I - D – MAJOR PERIODS AND STYLES OF ART

Place the periods listed below in their correct chronological order:

Baroque
Classical
Gothic
Hellenic [Greek]
Hellenistic [Greek-like]
Impressionism
Expressionism
Neo-Classical
Post-Impressionism
Realism
Renaissance
Rococo
Romanesque
Romanticism

01. ______________________

02. ______________________

03. ______________________

04. ______________________

05. ______________________

06. ______________________

07. ______________________

08. ______________________

09. ______________________

10. ______________________

11. ______________________

12. ______________________

13. ______________________

14. ______________________

FINAL REVIEW I - E – ARTISTS & MAJOR PERIODS OF ART

Place the below artists in their correct period of history:

Bernini	Constable	Friedrich	Manet	Seurat
Bosch	Courbet	Gauguin	Matisse	Titian
Botticelli	David	Géricault	Michelangelo	Turner
Boucher	Degas	Goya	Monet	Van Eyck
Bruegel	Duchamp	Hogarth	Picasso	Van Gogh
Caravaggio	Dürer	Kandinsky	Raphael	Velázquez
Cassatt	El Greco	Leonardo	Rembrandt	Vermeer
Cézanne	Fragonard	Magritte	Renoir	Watteau

1. RENAISSANCE:

____
____
____
____
____
____

2. NORTHERN RENAISSANCE:

____
____
____
____

3. MANNERISM

____

3. BAROQUE:

____
____
____
____
____

4. ROCOCO:

____
____
____
____

5. NEOCLASSICAL:

____

6. ROMANTICISM:

____
____
____
____
____

7. REALISM:

____

8. IMPRESSIONISM:

____
____
____
____
____

9. POST-IMPRESSIONISM:

____
____
____
____

10. TWENTIETH CENTURY:

- **Fauvism** ____________________
- **Cubism** ____________________
- **Dadaism** ____________________
- **Surrealism** ____________________
- **Abstract** ____________________

FINAL REVIEW II – ARCHITECTURE

Match the buildings below with the city in which they are located:

01. _____	Sphinx & Pyramid, c. 2500 B.C.E.	A. Aachen
02. _____	Ziggurat, c. 2100 B.C.E.	B. Agra
03. _____	Palace of Minos, c. 1600-1400 B.C.E.	C. Athens
04. _____	Parthenon, c. 438 B.C.E.	D. Chartres
05. _____	Altar of Zeus, c. 180 B.C.E.	E. Constantinople
06. _____	Pantheon, c. C.E. 126	F. Giza
07. _____	Hagia Sophia, 537	G. Granada, Spain
08. _____	San Vitale, 547	H. Knossus
09. _____	Chapel of Charlemagne, c. 800	I. London
10. _____	Notre Dame Cathedral, 1195 – 1220	J. New York
11. _____	Sainte Chapelle, 1243 – 1248	K. Paris, Medieval
12. _____	Palace of the Alhambra, 1200 – 1300	L. Paris, Belle Epoque
13. _____	Pazzi Chapel (Brunelesschi), 1430 – 1433	M. Paris, Contemporary
14. _____	Sistine Chapel (ceiling), 1512	N. Florence
15. _____	Taj Mahal, 1632 – 1647	O. Pergamun
16. _____	Piazza of St. Peter's, 1667	P. Ravenna
17. _____	Palace of Louis XIV, 1678	Q. Rome, Ancient
18. _____	Houses of Parliament, 1836 –1860	R. Rome, Renaissance
19. _____	Eiffel Tower, 1889	S. Rome, Baroque
20. _____	Seagram Building, 1958	T. Ur
21. _____	Pompidou Museum, 1977	U. Versailles
22. _____	Vietnam Veterans Memorial, 1982	V. Washington, D.C.

FINAL REVIEW III – LITERATURE AND FILM

Match the author or artist with their work:

01.	_______	Anonymous	A.	*Aeneid*
02.	_______	Homer	B.	*Animal Farm*
03.	_______	Sappho	C.	*Antigone*
04.	_______	Aeschylus	D.	*Book of the Courtier*
05.	_______	Sophocles	E.	*Candide*
06.	_______	Herodotus	F.	*Canterbury Tales*
07.	_______	Thucydides	G.	*City of God; Confessions*
08.	_______	Plato	H.	*City of Ladies*
09.	_______	Vergil	I.	*Color Purple*
10.	_______	Augustine	J.	*Communist Manifesto*
11.	_______	Benedict	K.	*Crime and Punishment*
12.	_______	Hrosvitha	L.	*Death of A Salesman*
13.	_______	Abelard	M.	*Divine Comedy*
14.	_______	Aquinas	N.	*Doll's House*
15.	_______	Dante	O.	*Don Quixote*
16.	_______	Chaucer	P.	*Encyclopédie*
17.	_______	Christine de Pisan	Q.	*Essay Concerning Human Understanding*
18.	_______	Pico della Mirandola	R.	*Essays*
19.	_______	Erasmus	S.	*Faust*
20.	_______	Machiavelli	T.	*Gilgamesh*
21.	_______	Castiglione	U.	*Hamlet*
22.	_______	Montaigne	V.	*History of Persian Wars*
23.	_______	Shakespeare	W.	*History of the Peloponnesian Wars*
24.	_______	Cervantes	X.	*Human Comedy*
25.	_______	Hobbes	Y.	*Iliad*
26.	_______	Milton	Z.	*In Praise of Folly*
27.	_______	Locke	AA.	*Interpretation of Dreams*
28.	_______	Diderot	BB.	*Leviathan*
29.	_______	Voltaire	CC.	*Moby Dick*
30.	_______	Rousseau	DD.	*Oliver Twist*
31	_______	Goethe	EE.	*Oration on Dignity of Man*
32	_______	Dickens	FF.	Oresteia Trilogy
33	_______	Melville	GG.	*Paradise Lost*
34	_______	Thoreau	HH.	*Poems*
35.	_______	Marx	II.	*Potemkin*
36.	_______	Balzac	JJ.	*The Prince*
37.	_______	Tolstoy	KK.	*Remembrance of Things Past*
38.	_______	Dostoyesky	LL.	*The Republic*
39	_______	Ibsen	MM.	*Rule (Regulations)*
40.	_______	Freud	NN.	"The Second Coming"
41.	_______	Proust	OO.	*Sic et Non (Yes and No)*
42	_______	Yeats	PP.	*Social Contract*
43.	_______	Kafka	QQ.	Summa Theologica
44	_______	Orwell, George	RR.	*Theophilus*
45	_______	Miller, Arthur	SS.	*The Trial*
46	_______	Beckett, Samuel	TT.	*Triumph of the Will; Olympia*
47	_______	Walker, Alice	UU.	*Waiting for Godot*
48.	_______	Eisenstein, Sergei	VV.	*Walden*
49.	_______	Riefenstahl, Leni	WW.	*War and Peace*
50.	_______	Bergman, Ingmar	XX.	*Wild Strawberries; 7th Seal*

FINAL REVIEW IV – TERMS

Match the definitions with the correct terms:

_____	A.	A speech unheard by other actors	01.	*a capella*
_____	B.	A standard or rule	02.	Academy
_____	C.	Age of Reason	03.	acropolis
_____	D.	Ancient Egyptian writing	04.	atrium
_____	E.	Ancient Mesopotamian writing	05.	Baroque
_____	F.	Aristocratic, frivolous art of the 1700s	06.	Basilica
_____	G.	Art style of Géricault, Friedrich, Blake	07.	*Belle Époque*
_____	H.	Belief in one god	08.	Canon
_____	I.	Box or shrine holding a sacred relic	09.	Capital
_____	J.	Bishop's throne	10.	Caryatid
_____	K.	Central portion of a church	11.	Catharsis
_____	L.	Dots of pure color, by Seurat	12.	*Cathedra*
_____	M.	Dramatic purging (Aristotle)	13.	*Chiaroscuro*
_____	N.	Dream-like paintings of Dali	14.	Classical
_____	O.	"Effortless grace"	15.	Codex
_____	P.	Emotional art of the 1600s	16.	Colonnade
_____	Q.	Excessive pride	17.	Cubism
_____	R.	Grammar, Rhetoric, Logic	18.	Cuneiform
_____	S.	Greco-Roman philosophy of pleasure	19.	Doric
_____	T.	Greek city-state	20.	Enlightenment
_____	U.	Greco-Roman philosophy of virtue and self control	21.	Epicureanism
_____	V.	Greek and Roman civilization	22.	Fauvism
_____	W.	Head of a column	23.	Fresco
_____	X.	"Keep death before your eyes"	24.	Hieroglyphics
_____	Y.	Image	25.	Hubris
_____	Z.	Large Roman hall used for meetings	26.	Icon
_____	AA.	Large, open public square (in Italy)	27.	*Kouros*
_____	BB.	Light/dark contrasts in painting	28.	*Memento Mori*
_____	CC.	Manuscript volume in pages	29.	Monotheism
_____	DD.	Mesopotamian stepped pyramid	30.	Nave
_____	EE.	Multi-dimensional art of Braque & Picasso	31.	Neolithic
_____	FF.	Music sung without instruments	32.	*Opus Dei*
_____	GG.	"New birth" or rebirth	33.	Piazza
_____	HH.	Open courtyard	34.	Pointillism
_____	II.	New Stone Age (birth of agriculture)	35.	*Polis*
_____	JJ.	Painting by wild beasts such as Matisse	36.	Relief
_____	KK.	Painting on fresh plaster	37.	Reliquary
_____	LL.	Part of cruciform church at right angles to the nave	38.	Renaissance
_____	MM.	Plato's School	39.	Rococo
_____	NN.	Row of columns	40.	Romanticism
_____	OO.	Sculpture attached to stone background	41.	Soliloquy
_____	PP.	Sculptured female figure used as a column	42.	*Sprezzatura*
_____	QQ.	Simplest order of Greek architecture	43.	Stoicism
_____	RR.	Site of the Parthenon	44.	Surrealism
_____	SS.	Spirals atop an Ionic capital	45.	Transept
_____	TT.	Standing male statue, usually nude	46.	Triptych
_____	UU.	The "Beautiful Age" (c. 1890-1914)	47.	Trivium
_____	VV.	Three-paneled painting	48.	Trope
_____	WW.	Words added to melismas	49.	Volutes
_____	XX.	"Work of God"	50.	Ziggurat

FINAL REVIEW V – ASIA, ISLAM, AFRICA

Match the definitions with the correct answers:

01.	_____	Important city of Indus River Civilization	A.	*Ahimsa*
02.	_____	Classical language of India	B.	Akbar
03.	_____	Oldest religious texts of India	C.	Akira Kurosawa
04.	_____	Oldest of the Hindu epics	D.	Alhambra
05.	_____	Greatest Hindu epic; 100,000 verses	E.	*Allah*
06.	_____	Most famous section of *Mahabharata*	F.	Ashoka
07.	_____	Oldest religion of India	G.	Babur
08.	_____	"Action" and its consequences on future lives	H.	*Baghavad-Gita*
09.	_____	Duty and moral responsibilities in Hinduism	I.	Baghdad
10.	_____	Teacher of the Four Noble Truths	J.	Beijing
11.	_____	Buddhist extinction of desire and suffering	K.	Calligraphy
12.	_____	Emperor spreading Buddhism beyond India	L.	Chinua Achebe
13.	_____	Buddhist religious shrines and reliquaries	M.	Confucius
14.	_____	Doctrine of nonviolence in Buddhism	N.	*Dharma*
15.	_____	Empire ruled by Chandra Gupta II	O.	Friday
16.	_____	Indian Classical writer of *Sakuntala*	P.	Gandhi
17.	_____	Country of origin of "Arabic" numbers	Q.	Gupta
18.	_____	Best known Chinese sage	R.	*Haiku*
19.	_____	Book of wisdom associated with Lao-tse	S.	*Hegira*
20.	_____	First Emperor of China	T.	Hinduism
21.	_____	Muslim name for God	U.	India
22.	_____	Messenger and prophet of Islam	V.	Kalidasa
23.	_____	Holy book of Islam	W.	*Karma*
24.	_____	Event marking year one of Muslim calendar	X.	Kyoto
25.	_____	Muslim building used for worship	Y.	*Mahabharata*
26.	_____	Special day of prayer for Muslims	Z.	Mohammed
27.	_____	"Beautiful writing"	AA.	Mohenjo-Daro
28.	_____	City of "House of Wisdom," Abbasid Dynasty	BB.	Mosque
29.	_____	Muslim palace in Granada, Spain	CC.	*Negritude*
30.	_____	Year *Reconquista* ended in Spain	DD.	*Nirvana*
31.	_____	Mystical branch of Islam	EE.	Opium
32.	_____	Afghan Founder of Mughal Empire	FF.	*Qurán / Koran*
33.	_____	Greatest Ruler of the Mughal Empire	GG.	*Ramayana*
34.	_____	Most beautiful Mughal building	HH.	*Samurai*
35.	_____	Indian nationalist leader using "nonviolence"	II.	Sanskrit
36.	_____	"Forbidden City" and "Imperial City" of China	JJ.	Satjayit Ray
37.	_____	Subject of 1839-1842 war with China	KK.	Shih Huang-ti
38.	_____	Traditional capital of Japan	LL.	Shinto
39.	_____	Religion native to Japan	MM.	Siddhartha Gautama
40.	_____	Japanese novel (c. 1015) by Lady Murasaki	*NN.*	Stupas
41.	_____	Japanese professional warrior	*OO.*	Sufism
42.	_____	Japanese Buddhism; sudden insights	*PP.*	Taj Mahal
43	_____	Japanese poetry in 3 lines and 17 syllables	QQ.	*Tao te ching*
44.	_____	Great stone ruins in southern Africa	RR.	*Tale of Genji*
45.	_____	Literary movement of Leopold Senghor	SS.	Vedas
46.	_____	African novelist, *Thing Fall Apart*, 1958	*TT.*	Wole Soyinka
47.	_____	African winner Nobel Prize for Literature, 1986	UU.	Zen
48.	_____	Japanese director of *Rashomon*, 1950	VV.	Zhang Yimou
49.	_____	Indian director of *The Apu Trilogy*, 1955-58	*WW.*	Zimbabwe
50.	_____	Chinese director of *Story of Qui Ju*, 1992	XX.	1492

APPENDIX A: LIBRARY ORIENTATION

Student's Name:
Row and Seat Number:

01. Visit the campus Library or Learning Resources Center (LRC) and learn the location of the items listed below. On the back of this page draw a map to show the location of:

    A. Card Catalog or Electronic Catalog of Library Holdings
    B. General Circulation Books
    C. Reference Books
    D. Current Newspapers
    E. Microfilm and Microfiche Area
    F. DVDs, CD-ROMS and Videotape Collection
    G. DVDs, CD-ROMS and Videotape Viewing Area
    H. Computer Stations
    I. Student Study Rooms
    J. Special Collections

02. In the General Circulation area, where are the locations of books with the below subjects? (You may find it helpful to draw a diagram.)

    – History?
    – Music?
    – Architecture?
    – Sculpture?
    – Painting?
    – Literature?

03. During what hours is the Library open?

    – Monday – Thursday?
    – Friday?
    – Saturday?
    – Sunday?

BONUS: In the Microfilm Area, what was the headline on page one of *The New York Times* for the day on which you were born? (Attach a printed copy made from the microfilm reader/printer.)

APPENDIX B: FINDING LIBRARY INFORMATION - BOOKS, PERIODICALS, AND AUDIOVISUAL MATERIALS

To find information on the humanities in the library, use the traditional card catalog (if it is still available) or better, use an electronic information network such as LINCCWeb. The Library Information Network Community Colleges is a state-funded information network that joins together the libraries of Florida's 28 community colleges. LINCCWeb provides convenient access to online library catalogs, reference materials, newspapers, and electronic databases. (The following information is taken from the LINCC FAQ /Frequently Asked Questions page.)

LINCCWeb can also be accessed by using any computer. Access to most of LINCCWeb's resources is free. However, access to some of its resources such as full-text databases is limited to registered community college students, faculty, and staff with a valid borrower ID. Your browser must be JAVAScript-enabled and able to accept cookies. The URL is www.ccla.lib.fl.us

LINCCWeb provides two separate search engines—"LINCCSearch" and "LINCCPlus"— designed to assist in searching for library materials and databases.

- **LINCCSearch** - Community College Library Catalogs - You can search for materials in your own college's library or statewide using Use LINCCSearch. (Reciprocal borrowing agreements exist between all community colleges and state universities in Florida. If you are a currently enrolled student, or a faculty or staff member at a community college, you may go to any other community college or state university library and borrow circulating books from them. You must have a valid library card and be in good standing with your home library in order to use this service.)
- **LINCCPlus** - Databases – You can simultaneously search up to seven databases at one time. Select from LINCCPlus' preset categories of databases or build your own personalized list of databases to search.

    - Academic Search Premier: Full-text information from a wide range of academic areas including business, social sciences, humanities, general academic, general science, and education. These databases include *Arts & Humanities Search (OCLC FirstSearch), Humanities Abstract, Readers Guide to Periodical Literature, ArticleFirst, Biography Index,* and *American Humanities Index*.
    - Newspapers: Full-text access to more than 100 newspapers, including Florida newspapers, and national, and international newspapers. ("Full-text" is essentially an article's text only [no graphics]. With full-text capability, you can view an entire article; not just a summary of an article.)

APPENDIX C: HUMANITIES INTERNET RESEARCH

GOALS OF THIS ASSIGNMENT:

1) To explore information about the Humanities available on the Internet,
2) To compare search engines and browsers such as GOOGLE, YAHOO!, MSN SEARCH, and ASK JEEVES.

SELECT A SUBJECT

Chose one of the below artists for your research.

____ Jacob Lawrence
____ Faith Ringgold
____ Mark Tansey
____ Rachel Whitehead
____ Jaune Quick-to-See Smith

COMPARE SEARCH ENGINES

Begin with a search for sites on the "Web, then do a search for "Images".

	Number of Web Sites Found	URL of Web Site first on the list *	Number of Images Found
- GOOGLE www.google.com			
- YAHOO! www.yahoo.com			
- MSN SEARCH search.msn.com/			
- ASK JEEVES www.ask.com/			

VISIT ONE WEB SITE FROM EACH SEARCH ENGINE

	Title of Web Site Visited	Your Evaluation of the Site
- GOOGLE		
- YAHOO!		
- MSN SEARCH		
- ASK JEEVES		

SUMMARY

In your opinion, which was the best search engine? Why?

APPENDIX D: EVALUATING MUSEUM WEB SITES

Evaluate the web sites of major museums in the United States and in Europe. Select two museums in the U.S.A. and one in Europe.

1. Which three museums did you select? Why?

   a)

   b)

   c)

2. What did you like or dislike about each museum's site?

   a)

   b)

   c)

3. How could the sites be improved?

4. Was it possible to search the museum's collections? By individual artists?

5. Which museum site did you prefer? Why?

U.S.A. MUSEUM SITES

METROPOLITAN MUSEUM OF ART, NEW YORK	www.metmuseum.org/
NATIONAL GALLERY OF ART, WASHINGTON, D.C.	www.nga.gov/
MUSEUM OF MODERN ART, NEW YORK	www.moma.org/
ART INSTITUTE OF CHICAGO	www.artic.edu/
NATIONAL MUSEUM OF AFRICAN ART, WASHINGTON, D.C.	www.nmafa.si.edu/default.htm
MUSEUM OF FINE ARTS, BOSTON	www.mfa.org/
LACMA: LOS ANGELES COUNTY MUSEUM OF ART	www.lacma.org/
NATIONAL GALLERY, LONDON	www.nationalgallery.org.uk/
TATE GALLERY [TATE BRITAIN, TATE MODERN], LONDON	www.tate.org.uk/
THE LOUVRE, PARIS	www.louvre.fr/louvrea.htm

APPENDIX E: WRITING YOUR HUMANITIES PAPER

One purpose of writing a research paper is to increase your ability to do research, specifically: (a) to find information, (b) to evaluate and then select meaningful information, and (c) to organize and communicate your results in writing that is clear and interesting. Your research should result also in a greater understanding of your subject, e.g., an artist's life and work.

Scholarship. Your research should be based on a variety of sources, not just one or two books or articles. Your paper should demonstrate your ability to unearth a variety of sources including books, magazine and newspaper articles, videotapes, DVDs, and sources on the Internet. If at all possible, your paper should include one "original source," that is a "first-hand" or "eyewitness" account.

Citations. Cite your sources of information using a brief citation at the end of each paragraph, and a complete citation in your Bibliography. All quotations and paraphrases must be cited. Here are some examples of complete citations:

BOOKS: Marling, Karal Ann, *Norman Rockwell*, New York: Taschen, 2005
ARTICLES: Patricia Jones, "The Art of Picasso," *Newsweek*, January 10, 2000, p. 86.
WEB SITES: Alice Smith, "The Genius of Picasso," MASTERS OF ART, <u>http://www.cas.usf.edu/english/walker/mla.html</u>
Your Web citations must include: a) author's name, b) title of the work in quotation marks, c) title of the Web page capitalized, d) full http address [underlined], and e) the date you visited the site.

Plagiarism. Beware the temptation to copy your report from a book or from the Internet. Your challenge is not to copy from someone else but to put the facts and ideas you've found *into your own words.* Use quotation marks if using an author's exact words. Changing just a few words around is still plagiarism, even if you cite the source of your information. Plagiarism detected may result in a "F" for your report and a lowering of the final course grade.

Good Writing. Good writing is *simple, clear,* and *forceful.* Remember to use your paragraphs to organize your thoughts effectively. Be sure you understand what you have written. Beware using vocabulary or phrases that are not clear to you and that you may not be able to explain.

Use standard spelling and punctuation. Reduce spelling or typing mistakes by having your paper proofread by someone else or using computer software ("Spell-check"). Review the guidelines for writing essays and research papers in the Appendix of the Simon and Schuster *Handbook for Writers* or a similar book.

Content and format.

1. Your paper should be typed and double-spaced.

2. Your research paper must be a minimum of 1,500 words and no more than 2,000 words so the quality and not just the quantity of your work can be evaluated.

3. Your paper should answer the questions on the next page. One format for your paper could be to begin each paragraph with a question, followed by your answer, and then the source of your information. Be sure to cite your source of information at the end of each paragraph. *Use short citations* (author, title, page number) since your complete citations will be in your Bibliography(see below).

4. Prepare and include a cover page showing: (1) your name, (2) the section number of your class, (3) your row and seat number, (4) the title, and (5) the number of words in your report. Please staple your pages together in the upper left-hand corner. Keep a backup copy of your paper on a computer disc.

SUGGESTED OUTLINE AND POSSIBLE QUESTIONS TO ANSWER

I: LIFE OF AN ARTIST and BIBLIOGRAPHY (750 words)

A. BIOGRAPHY

1. What was the most significant *short* (one or two sentences) statement made about the artist or quotation made by the artist?
2. When and where was the artist born and when and where did the artist die?
3. What was the *first* important work of art by this artist and *why* was it important?
4. Which work is considered to be his or her "masterpiece"? Why?
5. What four other important works were created by the artist and *why* were they important?
6. What were the most important characteristics of the works created by the artist (style, techniques, subject matter)?
7. What was interesting or meaningful *to you* about the artist?

B. ANNOTATED BIBLIOGRAPHY - List at least *fifteen* sources of information, using these categories: A) books, B) articles, C) web pages, and D) other sources. Please use complete citations. *Evaluate* at least *ten* items with comments or annotations of one or two sentences evaluating their strengths or weaknesses. Bibliographies without evaluations or comments may receive a lower grade.

II: WORKS OF THE ARTIST: SEEING AND INTERPRETING (750 words)

A. DESCRIPTION AND ANALYSIS OF SPECIFIC WORKS - *In your own words*, describe in detail and discuss three or four works of the artist. Be sure to cite the source of your information at the end of each paragraph, unless it is *your own description or analysis*.

1. What one work by the artist did you like the most? (*Describe the work in detail.*)
2. Why did you like this work?
3. What interesting *details* about this work did you discover after carefully studying and reading about it (especially any details not noticed at first glance)?
4. What did you discover about the *meaning* of this work by carefully looking and thinking about it, or by reading about it?
5. What did you learn from your research about the meaning and significance of two or three other works by the artist? [Describe and interpret.]

B. ILLUSTRATIONS - Attach illustrations (black and white, or in color) of each of the works you've selected.

C. SUMMARY - What was the single most important thing you learned from doing this assignment?

D. WORKS CITED – List (without comment) all works *actually used* for Part II of this paper.

Remember your goal is to present a paper that is well written, uses your own words (not copied), is interesting, and is based on a variety of sources.

APPENDIX F: FILM ESSAY (500 – 750 Words)

1. INTRODUCTION:

The purposes of writing this essay are to:

(a) organize and clarify your thoughts on the film you've selected,
(b) further your understanding of movies as an art form,
(c) learn more about the values of the culture depicted in the film, and perhaps
(d) increase your understanding of yourself.

2. SOME QUESTIONS TO ANSWER:

A. Description of the Film:

1. What story was told by the film (one or two paragraphs only, please)?
2. What was the first scene in the film and why was it important?
3. What was the most significant statement made by any character in the film? What character made the statement?
4. What was the most meaningful scene in the film?
5. What was the final scene in the film and why was it significant?

B. Critique:

1. What did you like the most about the film? What did you like the least about the film?
2. What was the message or theme of the film? Did the title of the film have any meaning? If so, what was its meaning?
3. What values did the film support? What values did it question?
4. Was there anything unusual or perplexing about the film?
5. What did you learn from viewing this film (especially your increased understanding of life in other cultures, or your better appreciation of what it's like to be human)?

OPTIONAL QUESTIONS (for those desiring an above average grade):

A. What information did you acquire from reading a review of your movie? (Be sure to attach a copy of the full review to your essay.)

You can use the Internet to find a review of the film you've watched. One good source for reviews is "The Internet Movie Database." The address is **http://www.imdb.com/** Another good source are the thoughtful reviews of Roger Ebert **http://rogerebert.suntimes.com/apps/pbcs.dll/frontpage** or the "Reel Views" of James Berardinelli **http://movie-reviews.colossus.net/**

B. What questions were raised in your mind while watching the film? <u>List</u> your questions; they do not have to be answered in this essay. (If Aristotle was right in saying "all knowledge begins with wonder," then your questions will suggest how much you have gained by thoughtfully watching the film.)

3. SOME ADVICE:

a. Be sure to take notes while watching the film.
b. Your report should be in correct standard English usage (including spelling and punctuation). Try to write plainly and simply.
c. Type your paper. Then, carefully proofread it. Keep a backup copy on your computer.
d. Beware of plagiarism; don't take someone else's ideas or words without giving that person credit. Therefore, cite your sources and use quotations marks as necessary.
e. Type your name, row & seat number, and section number in the upper right hand corner of the first page. Please, staple your paper in the upper left-hand corner.

FILMS ON DVD AND VIDEOTAPE

OSAMA (Mohsen Makhmalbaf)	Afghanistan	2003	82"
CHUQUIAGO	Bolivia	1977	87"
CENTRAL STATION [NR] (Walter Salles)	Brazil	1998	115"
PYGMALION	Britain	1948	96"
THE THIRD MAN (Carol Reed)	Britain	1949	104"
KEÏTA: THE HERITAGE OF THE GRIOT	Burkina Faso	1995	94"
JESUS OF MONTREAL [R]	Canada	1989	119"
THE STORY OF QUI JU [NR]	China	1992	100"
TO LIVE (Zhang Yimou) [R]	China	1994	130"
PIECES OF IDENTITY [NR]	Congo/Belgium	1998	93"
STRAWBERRY AND CHOCOLATE [R]	Cuba	1994	110"
GUANTANAMERA (Tomas Gutierrez Alea)	Cuba	1997	104"
LOVES OF A BLONDE (Milos Forman)	Czech	1965	88"
BABETTE'S FEAST (Gabriel Axel)	Denmark	1987	102"
RULES OF THE GAME (Jean Renoir)	France	1939	110"
400 BLOWS (Truffaut)	France	1959	99"
JEAN DE FLORETTE (Claude Berri)	France	1986	122"
RENDEZVOUS IN PARIS [NR] (Eric Rohmer)	France	1996	100"
AMELIE (Jean-Pierre Jeunet) [R]	France	2001	121"
THE LAST LAUGH (F.W. Murnau)	Germany	1924	72"
PANDORA's BOX (F.W. Murnau)	Germany	1928	110"
THE BLUE ANGEL (Joseph von Sternberg)	Germany	1930	98"
THE NASTY GIRL (Verhoeven)	Germany	1990	96"
PATHER PANCHALI (Satyajit Ray)	India	1954	112"
MONSOON WEDDING (Mira Nair)	India	2002	114"
GABBEH [NR]	Iran	1996	75"
CHILDREN OF HEAVEN (Majid Majidi) [PG]	Iran	1998	87"
LA STRADA (Fellini)	Italy	1954	107"
THE BICYCLE THIEF (De Sica)	Italy	1949	90"
GOSPEL ACCORDING TO ST MATTHEW	Italy	1964	136"
THE BATTLE OF ALGIERS (Pontocorvo)	Italy/Algeria	1965	123"
TREE OF WOODEN CLOGS (Olmi)	Italy	1978	185"
GUIMBA THE TYRANT (Chieck Omar Sisoko)	Mali	1995	93"
LIKE WATER FOR CHOCOLATE	Mexico	1993	113"
THE WHALE RIDER (Niki Caro)	New Zealand	2003	101"
CHARACTER/KARAKTER (Mike van Diem) [R]	Netherlands	1998	120"
SPRING SUMMER FALL WINTER ... AND SPRING	South Korea	2003	106"
RASHOMON (Kurosawa)	Japan	1951	83"
SEVEN SAMURAI (Kurosawa)	Japan	1954	197"
TAMPOPO (Itami)	Japan	1987	95"
MAN OF MARBLE (Wajda)	Poland	1977	160"
THE DECALOGUE (Kieslowski) [Try one episode]	Poland	1998	550"
MOOLAADÉ (Sembène Ousmane) [NR]	Senegal	2004	124"
VIRIDIANA (Bunuel)	Spain	1961	90"
ALL ABOUT MY MOTHER [R] (Almodóvar)	Spain	1999	101"
SAWDUST AND TINSEL (Bergman)	Sweden	1953	95"
THE SEVENTH SEAL (Bergman)	Sweden	1956	96"
YOL	Turkey	1983	111"
THE GOLD RUSH (Chaplin)	USA	1924	81"
THE GENERAL (Buster Keaton)	USA	1927	74"
ALL QUIET ON THE WESTERN FRONT	USA	1930	105"
CITIZEN KANE (Orson Welles)	USA	1941	119"
DO THE RIGHT THING [R] (Spike Lee)	USA	1989	120"
MY FAMILY (MI FAMILIA) [R] (Gregory Nava)	USA	1995	128"

APPENDIX G: MUSEUM VISIT (750 words)

A. THE MOST BEAUTIFUL OBJECT IN THE MUSEUM

1. Begin by walking through the museum. You are seeking the most *beautiful* object in the museum. When you have discovered it, stand or sit before it for at least two minutes!
2. Try not at first to look at the "title" or other information displayed with the object. Use your insight and imagination to understand the art before you.
3. Look at it with care. If possible, "listen" to it and hear what the artist is trying to communicate. Think about what thoughts and questions are going through your mind as you watch it.
4. Now begin to write your report. Try to express your thoughts plainly and simply using correct standard English. *Be sure to include*:
   a) the title of the work you've selected and its artist.
   b) a detailed description of the work.
   c) the feelings the work aroused in you.
   d) a list of the questions you thought about while watching it.
   e) a sketch (8x10) of the work of art, including the important details. [YES, the sketch is important!]

B. THE MOST INTERESTING ART FROM ASIA, AFRICA, OR LATIN AMERICA

a) Name the most *interesting* non-European work of art in the museum.
b) Describe the work and why you selected it.

C. SPECIAL EXHIBITION(S) <u>(FOR AN ABOVE AVERAGE OR EXCELLENT GRADE)</u>

a) What was the title of the special exhibition(s)?
b) What was the purpose of the exhibition(s)?
c) What did you learn about the general subject of the special exhibition(s)?
d) Which one work in the exhibition(s) *appealed* to you? *WHY?*

FINAL CHECKLIST

a) Has your report been typed?
b) Has it been proofread (don't forget to use "spell check" and "grammar check")?
c) Are the pages in order and have they been stapled?
d) Have you placed in the upper-right hand corner of the first page: (1) your name? (2) row & seat number? (3) the total number of words in your paper

MUSEUM POLICIES AND RULES OF CONDUCT

Museums and galleries are concerned about both the exhibition and the protection of the works of art in their collections. Knowing and observing the below rules will be helpful.

1. PLEASE DO NOT TOUCH ANY WORKS OF ART. Try to keep at least eight inches away to avoid any accidental damage. Be prepared for a gallery attendant to remind if you get too close.
2. APPROPRIATE BEHAVIOR. Eating, drinking, gum chewing, and smoking are not permitted in the galleries. Running, jumping, and physically fooling around are not permitted because of the hazard they create for the artwork and for other visitors. Children are welcome, but their behavior should be monitored by adult companions.
3. NO PHOTOGRAPHY / VIDEOGRAPHY. Cameras and video recorders may not be permitted in the museum. ASK FIRST. Flash photography, videography and the use of tripods are almost always prohibited.
4. HANDICAPPED ACCESSIBILITY. Reserved parking, wheelchairs and elevator are available. Inquire at the front desk for assistance.
5. STUDENT DISCOUNTS. Ask at the front desk if student discounts are available. (Be sure to have your student ID with you.)

APPENDIX H: AUDIO DRAMA ON THE INTERNET

AUDIO DRAMA ON THE BBC (BRITISH BROADCASTING CORPORATION)

Here's an opportunity to listen to a broadcast of a radio play by the British Broadcasting Corporation (BBC) via audio streaming on the internet. Most of the plays are archived for seven days after their broadcast, so you can listen to them easily at your convenience. *Please note that listening to an audio drama is likely to require more attention than watching TV.*
Give it your undivided attention for 45 to 60 minutes in order to "see" and understand the play.

BBC RADIO 7 **http://www.bbc.co.uk/bbc7/**

BBC 7, the newest BBC Radio station, features entertainment programs, including mysteries, science fiction, comedy, and daily dramas for seven hours each day.

- "Listen Live" using Real Player or Windows Media Player: **http://www.bbc.co.uk/bbc7/**
- "Listen Again" (the last seven days): **http://www.bbc.co.uk/bbc7/listenagain/saturday/**
- The BBC Radio Player is available at: **http://www.bbc.co.uk/radio/aod/bbc7.shtml**
- For help in listening: **http://www.bbc.co.uk/bbc7/help/**

BBC RADIO 4 – ARTS AND DRAMA **http://www.bbc.co.uk/radio4/arts/**

Use the above URL to visit the BBC Radio 4 "Listen Again – Arts and Drama" page. CLICK on one of options listed for information about the plays and to listen to a play of your choice.

- AFTERNOON PLAY (45 minutes
- SATURDAY PLAY (60 minutes)
- FRIDAY PLAY (60 minutes)
- CLASSIC SERIAL (60 minutes

BBC RADIO 3 -- DRAMA ON 3
http://www.bbc.co.uk/radio3/dramaon3/

Full-length, intellectually-challenging plays from Euripedes' *Medea to* Thomas Mann's *Magic Mountain,* including new specially commissioned works from Caryl Churchill and Shelagh Stevenson.

BBC WORLD SERVICE - PLAY OF THE WEEK
http://www.bbc.co.uk/worldservice/programmes/play_of_the_week.shtml

Use the above URL above to reach the Home Page of the BBC World Service Play of the Week. Then CLICK on "Listen to Play of the Week" to hear the play.

Your Assignment:
Listen to one of the plays, then, in 500 to 750 words, answer these questions:

1. What was the title of the play, and who was the author? What was the significance of the title?
2. What were the important events in the story?
3. Who was the most important character in the play? Why was this character important?
4. Did the play give you something to think about? Did it have a message? Was it more than entertaining?
5. What was your personal reaction in listening to a play on the radio? Did the play interest you? Why, or why not?
6. What three questions came to your mind as you listened to the play? (You don't have to answer your three questions.)

APPENDIX I: RECOMMENDED BOOKS

General Works

Barzun, Jacques	FROM DAWN TO DECADENCE, 1500 TO THE PRESENT: 500 YEARS OF WESTERN CULTURAL LIFE (2000)
Beckett, Wendy	SISTER WENDY'S AMERICAN COLLECTION (2000)
Berger, John	WAYS OF SEEING (1973)
Boorstin, Daniel J.	THE CREATORS: A HISTORY OF HEROES OF THE IMAGINATION (1992)
Clark, Kenneth	CIVILIZATION (1971)
Denby, David	GREAT BOOKS: MY ADVENTURES WITH HOMER, ROUSSEAU, WOOLF, AND OTHER INDESTRUCTIBLE WRITERS OF THE WESTERN WORLD (1996)
Glancey, Jonathan	THE STORY OF ARCHITECTURE (2000)
Hagen, R. and R.	MASTERPIECES IN DETAIL: WHAT GREAT PAINTINGS SAY (2000)
Hughes, Robert	AMERICAN VISIONS (1997)
Strickland, Carol	THE ANNOTATED MONA LISA: A CRASH COURSE IN ART HISTORY FROM PREHISTORIC TO POST-MODERN (1992)
Ross, Nancy Wilson	WAYS OF ASIAN WISDOM: HINDUISM, BUDDHISM, AND ZEN, AND THEIR SIGNIFICANCE FOR THE WEST (1966)

Artists

The below books published by Taschen are fine sources of information. They are beautifully illustrated, reasonably priced, and short in length (less than 100 pages).

Frank Zöllner	LEONARDO (2000)
Barbara Deimling	SANDRO BOTTICELLI, 1444/45-1510 (1994)
Gilles Néret	MICHELANGELO: 1475-1564 (1998)
Walter Bosing	BOSCH, c. 1450-1516: BETWEEN HEAVEN AND HELL (1991)
R.M. and R. Hagen	PIETER BRUEGEL, c. 1525-1569: PEASANTS, FOOLS & DEMONS
John Berger	ALBRECHT DÜRER (1994)
Michael Bockemuhl	REMBRANDT (1992)
Norbert Schneider	VERMEER, 1632-1675: VEILED EMOTION (1999)
Norbert Wolf	VELÁZQUEZ (1999)
Michael Bockemuhl	TURNER, 1775-1851: WORLD OF LIGHT AND COLOUR (1993)

K. Sagner-Duchting	CLAUDE MONET, 1840-1926 (1994)
Peter H. Feist	PIERRE-AUGUSTE RENOIR, 1841-1919 (1993)
Bernd Growe	EDGAR DEGAS, 1834-1917 (1992)
Ingo F. Walther	VINCENT VAN GOGH, 1853-1890: VISION AND REALITY (1990)
Ingo F. Walther	PAUL GAUGUIN, 1848-1903: PRIMITIVE SOPHISTICATE (1992)
Hajo Düchting	SEURAT (1999)
Cornelia Stabenow	HENRI ROUSSEAU, 1844-1910 (1991)
Ulrich Bischoff	EDVARD MUNCH, 1863-1944 (1990)
Gilles Neret	GUSTAV KLIMT, 1862-1918 (1993)
Renate Ulmer	ALFONS MUCHA: THE MASTER OF ART NOUVEAU (1994)
Walther & Metzger	MARC CHAGALL, 1887-1985: PAINTING AS POETRY (1993)
Hajo Duchting	ROBERT AND SONIA DELAUNAY: THE TRIUMPH OF COLOR (1994)
Andrea Kettenmann	FRIDA KAHLO, 1907-1954: PAIN AND PASSION (1993)
Andrea Kettenmann	DIEGO RIVERA, 1886-1957: A REVOLUTIONARY SPIRIT (1997)
Kranzfelder, Ivo	GEORGE GROSZ, 1893-1959 (1994)
Eva Karcher	OTTO DIX (1992)
Ingo F. Walther	PABLO PICASSO, 1881-1973: GENIUS OF THE CENTURY (1986)
Jacques Meuris	RENE MAGRITTE, 1898-1967 (1992)
Descharmes & Néret	SALVADOR DALÍ (1993)
Rolf G. Renner	EDWARD HOPPER, 1882-1967 (1990)
Britta Benke	GEORGIA O'KEEFFE, 1887-1986: FLOWERS IN THE DESERT
Jacob Baal-Teshuva	ALEXANDER CALDER (1998)
Klaus Honnef	ANDY WARHOL (1991)
Janis Hendrickson	ROY LICHTENSTEIN (1988)
Gilles Néret	BALTHUS (2003)
Karal Ann Marling	NORMAN ROCKWELL (2005)

APPENDIX J: STUDY CARDS

The following study cards are provided to emphasize learning the core content of an Introduction to the Humanities course. The card with its question is printed on the front of the page; the reverse of the page gives you space for your answer. Cut out the cards and use them for studying.

The running head at the top of the page tells you which area of the text is being tested.

STUDY CARDS - ANCIENT CIVILIZATIONS - A

World's oldest cave paintings	World's oldest statuette	World's first civilization
Capital city of Hammurabi	Type of writing used in ancient Mesopotamia	Stepped pyramid of Mesopotamia
First great epic hero; King of Uruk	Babylonian law code ("an eye for an eye")	Name of the first known architect in history
Egyptian pharaoh advocating monotheism	Capital city of Akhenaton	Ancient Egyptian Writing
Greatest city of Minoan civilization	Greek word for an independent city state	Greek marketplace and center for public meetings
Author of the *Iliad*	First known woman poet	Greek standing male statue, generally nude

STUDY CARDS - Place your answers in the spaces below.

_ _ _ _ _	_ _ _ _ _ _ _ _ _ _ _ _ _ _ _ _ _ _ _	_ _ _ _ _ _ _ _ _
_ _ _ _ _ _ _ _ _	_ _ _ _ _ _ _ _ _ _	_ _ _ _ _ _ _ _
_ _ _ _ _ _ _ _	_ _ _ _ _ _ _ _ _ _	_ _ _ _ _ _ _ _ _ _
_ _ _ _ _ _ _ _ _ _	_ _ _ _ _ _ _	_ _ _ _ _ _ _ _ _ _
_ _ _ _ _	_ _ _ _ _	_ _ _ _ _ _ _ _
_ _ _ _ _ _ _	_ _ _ _ _ _ _	_ _ _ _ _

STUDY CARDS - ANCIENT CIVILIZATIONS - B

Simplest order of Greek architecture	Order of of architecture with volutes	Order of architecture with acanthus leaves
Head or top of a column	Sculptor of *Aphrodite* *of Cyrene*	Greek word meaning rule or standard
Greek god of logic order and reason	Greek god of emotions and of wine	Greek work for excessive pride
Character flaw causing hero's tragic end	First Greek playwright (*Oresteia*) trilogy)	Author of *Oedipus the King* and *Antigone*
Playwright of comedies (*Lysistrata*)	First Greek historian (*The Persian Wars*)	First objective. scientific historian (*Peloponnesian Wars*)
Political leader during the Golden Age of Greece	Greek Presocratic philosopher "Man is the measure of all things"	Best known teacher of Plato

***STUDY CARDS* -** Place your answers in the spaces below. ✂

_ _ _ _ _ _ _ _ _ _	_ _ _ _ _	_ _ _ _ _
_ _ _ _ _	_ _ _ _ _ _ _ _ _ _	_ _ _ _ _ _ _
_ _ _ _ _ _	_ _ _ _ _ _ _	_ _ _ _ _ _
_ _ _ _ _ _ _ _ _	_ _ _ _ _ _ _ _ _	_ _ _ _ _ _ _ _
_ _ _ _ _ _ _ _ _ _	_ _ _ _ _ _ _ _ _	_ _ _ _ _ _ _ _ _ _ _ _
_ _ _ _ _ _ _ _	_ _ _ _ _ _ _ _ _ _	_ _ _ _ _ _ _ _

STUDY CARDS - ANCIENT CIVILIZATIONS - C

Greek philosopher of Ideal Reality	Best known student of Plato; founder of the Lyceum	Aristotle's term for the "purging" effect of tragedy
Most beautiful building of ancient Athens	Site of the Parthenon and highest point of the city	Sculptured female figures as columns
"Greek-like" civilization after Alexander the Great	Greatest city of the Hellenistic Age	Wealthiest city of Hellenistic Asia
Graeco-Roman philosophy emphasizing pleasure	Graeco-Roman philosophy emphasizing self control	Public meeting place of Rome
First great Emperor of Rome	Greatest Roman poet, author of the *Aeneid*	Roman building topped by a dome and an oculus
Most important city of the Eastern Roman Empire	Year of the last Roman emperor in the west	Year Constantinople fell to the Turks

STUDY CARDS - Place your answers in the spaces below.

STUDY CARDS – ANCIENT CIVILIZATIONS - D

Important cities of Indus River Valley Civilization	Classical language of India introduced by Aryan invaders	Oldest religious texts of India
Oldest of the Hindu epics	Greatest Hindu epic (100,000 verses)	Most famous part of the *Mahabharata*
Oldest religion of India	In Hinduism, "Actions" and their consequences on future lives	"Duty" and moral responsibilities in Hinduism
Founder of Buddhism	Buddhist term for "extinction" of desire and suffering	Hindu belief in the endless cycle of birth, death, and reincarnation
Buddhist religious shrines and reliquaries	Doctrine of nonviolence in Buddhism	Emperor spreading Buddhism beyond the borders of India
First important Chinese philosopher	Book of wisdom associated with Lao-tse	First Emperor of China

STUDY CARDS **-** Place your answers in the spaces below.

_ _ _ _ _	_ _ _ _ _ _ _ _	_ _ _ _ _ _ _ - _ _ _ _
_ _ _ _ _ _ _ _ - _ _ _ _	_ _ _ _ _ _ _ _ _ _ _	_ _ _ _ _
_ _ _ _ _ _	_ _ _ _ _	_ _ _ _ _ _ _ _
_ _ _ _ _ _ _	_ _ _ _	_ _ _ _ _ _ _
_ _ _ _ _ _	_ _ _ _ _ _	_ _ _ _ _ _
_ _ _ _ _ _ _	_ _ _ _ _ _ _ _	_ _ _ _ _

STUDY CARDS - THE MIDDLE AGES - A

Belief in one God	The "Good News" of Matthew, Mark, Luke and John	Two Greek letters used as a sign of Christianity
Roman building later used for churches	Long, central space of a church	The part of a church set at right angles to the nave
Open courtyard in a home or a church	Semicircular eastern end of a church	Row of windows in a wall above a roof
Emperor issuing edict of toleration in A.D. 312	Apostle spreading Christianity to the non-Jewish world of the Roman Empire	Most important church of Constantinople
Other name for the Eastern Roman Empire	Manuscript book bound with pages	Earliest New Testament in Greek
Book containing Augustine's linear view of history	Author of the *Confessions*	Author of *Consolation of Philosophy*

STUDY CARDS - Place your answers in the spaces below.

_ _ _ _ _ _	_ _ _ _ _ _	_ _ _ _ _ _ _ _ _ _
_ _ _ _ _ _ _ _	_ _ _ _	_ _ _ _ _ _ _ _
_ _ _ _ _ _ _ _ _ _	_ _ _ _	_ _ _ _ _ _
_ _ _ _ _ _ _ _ _ _ _	_ _ _ _	_ _ _ _ _ _ _ _ _ _ _
_ _ _ _ _ _ _ _ _ _ _ _ _ _ _	_ _ _ _ _	_ _ _ _ _ _ _ _ _ _ _ _ _ _ _
_ _ _ _ _ _ _ _	_ _ _ _ _ _ _ _ _	_ _ _ _ _ _ _ _ _

STUDY CARDS - THE MIDDLE AGES - B

Art consisting of small stones	Painting done on fresh plaster	Greek word for "image"
"Image Breaker"	Crowned emperor in A.D. 800	Capital city of Charlemagne
Important scholar at Aachen	Writing developed by Carolingian scholars	Medieval course of study consisting of grammar, rhetoric, and logic
Author of important monastic Rule	Medieval religious chant, usually sung plainsong	Art form associated with *Quem Queritas* trope
Name of the crusade against Muslim Spain	Country saving Aristotle's works	Oldest *chanson de geste*
Best-known medieval morality play	Most important style of architecture, 1000-1150	Most important style of architecture, 1150-1400

STUDY CARDS - Place your answers in the spaces below.

_ _ _ _	_ _ _ _ _ _	_ _ _ _ _ _
_ _ _ _ _ _	_ _ _ _ _ _ _ _ _ _ _	_ _ _ _ _ _ _ _ _ _
_ _ _ _ _ _ _	_ _ _ _ _ _ _ _ _	_ _ _ _ _ _
_ _ _ _ _	_ _ _ _ _ _ _ _ _	_ _ _ _ _ _ _ _
_ _ _ _ _ _ _ _ _ _ _ _	_ _ _ _ _	_ _ _ _ _ _ _ _ _ _ _
_ _ _ _ _ _	_ _ _ _ _ _ _ _ _ _	_ _ _ _ _ _ _ _

STUDY CARDS - THE MIDDLE AGES - C

Most important characteristic of Gothic architecture	Father of Gothic architecture	First Gothic Church
Meaning of the Latin words "Notre Dame"	Cathedral containing *Notre Dame de Belle Verriére*	Century of the "medieval renaissance"
First university in northern Europe	Important teacher of the University of Paris (*Sic et Non*, 1121)	Author of the *Summa Theologica*
Author of the *Divine Comedy* (Hell, Purgatory, Heaven)	Author of "And gladly would he learn and gladly teach"	Author of *The Book of the City of Ladies* (1404)
Realistic painter of the Arena Chapel frescoes in Padua (c. 1305)	Latin phrase meaning "Keep death before your eyes"	Founder of the Franciscan Order
Author of 300 sonnets to Laura; crowned poet Laureate in 1348	Painters of the *Trés Riches Heures du Duc de Berry* (1416)	Term meaning "new birth" or "renewal"

STUDY CARDS - Place your answers in the spaces below. ✂

_ _ _ _ _ _ _	_ _ _ _ _ _ _ _ _ _	_ _ _ _ _
_ _ _ _ _ _	_ _ _ _ _ _ _ _	_ _ _ _ _ _ _
_ _ _ _ _ _ _	_ _ _ _ _ _ _	_ _ _ _ _
_ _ _ _ _ _ _ _ _ _ _ _ _ _ _ _	_ _ _ _ _ _ _	_ _ _ _ _
_ _ _ _ _ _ _	_ _ _ _ _ _ _ _ _ _ _	_ _ _ _ _ _
_ _ _ _ _ _ _ _ _ _ _	_ _ _ _ _ _ _ _ _ _ _ _ _ _ _ _	_ _ _ _ _ _ _ _

STUDY CARDS - THE MIDDLE AGES - D - ISLAM

Muslim name for God	Messenger and prophet of Islam	Holy Book of Islam
Event marking year one of the Muslim calendar	Muslim building used for worship	Special day for prayer for Muslims
Muslim holy month of fasting	Word meaning "beautiful writing"	Intricate decorations of geometric designs and sacred texts
City of "House of Wisdom," Abbasid Dynasty	Country of origin of "Arabic" numerals	Mystical branch of Islam
Best known Sufi mystic poet	Muslim palace complex in Granada, Spain	Year the *Reconquista* ended in Spain
Afghan founder of the Mughal Empire	Greatest ruler of the Mughal Empire	Shah Jehan's beautiful Mughal building

STUDY CARDS - Place your answers in the spaces below. ✂

_ _ _ _ _	_ _ _ _ _ _ _ _ _	_ _ _ _ _
_ _ _ _ _ _	_ _ _ _ _ _	_ _ _ _ _ _
_ _ _ _ _ _ _ _ _ _ _	_ _ _ _ _ _	_ _ _ _ _
_ _ _ _	_ _ _ _ _	_ _ _ _ _ _ _ _
_ _ _ _	_ _ _ _ _ _ _ _ _	_ _ _ _
_ _ _ _ _ _ _ _	_ _ _ _ _	_ _ _ _ _

STUDY CARDS - EARLY MODERN EUROPE - A

Most important city of the Early Italian Renaissance	Sculptor of the Doors of Paradise, Florence Baptistery	Builder of the dome of Florence Cathedral
Leading patrons of Florence	Artist of *La Primavera* and *The Birth of Venus*	Multi-talented "Renaissance man" (Notebooks, Last Supper)
Sculptor of *David* (before the battle)	German inventor of printing with movable type	Florentine humanist (*Oration on the Dignity of Man*, 1486)
Machiavelli's book on how to get and keep power	Author of *The Book of the Courtier* (1528)	Term meaning "effortless mastery"
Monk opposed to the vanities of Renaissance Florence	Most important city of the High Renaissance	Leading patrons of Rome
Painter of the Sistine Chapel	Painter of the *School of Athens*	City of the Late Italian Renaissance known for its oil paintings

STUDY CARDS - Place your answers in the spaces below. ✂

_ _ _ _ _ _ _ _ _ _ _ _ _	_ _ _ _ _ _ _ _ _	_ _ _ _ _ _ _ _ _
_ _ _ _ _ _ _ _ _ _ _ _ _ _ _ _	_ _ _ _ _ _ _ _ _ _ _	_ _ _ _ _ _ _
_ _ _ _	_ _ _ _ _ _ _ _ _ _	_ _ _ _ _ _ _ _ _ _ _ _ _ _
_ _ _ _ _ _ _ _ _ _ _ _	_ _ _ _ _ _ _ _ _ _ _ _	_ _ _ _ _ _ _ _ _ _
_ _ _ _ _ _ _ _ _ _	_ _ _ _	_ _ _ _ _ _ _ _ _ _ _
_ _ _ _ _ _ _	_ _ _ _ _ _ _ _	_ _ _ _ _ _ _ _ _ _ _ _ _ _

STUDY CARDS - EARLY MODERN EUROPE - B

Early Venetian painter (*Le Concert Champêtre*)	Most famous painter of Renaissance Venice (*Venus of Urbino*)	Witness to the Arnolfini Marriage
Greatest German artist of the early 1500s (*Knight, Death, & Devil*)	German artist of the *Isenheim Altarpiece*	German religious reformer who questioned indulgences in 1517
Leader of the Protestant Reformation in Geneva	Christian Humanist of early 1500s (*In Praise of Folly*)	Netherlandish artist of demons and earthly delights
Netherlandisch painter of peasants and proverbs	Greatest playwright of Elizabethan England	Speech unheard by other actors in a play
Word used by Montaigne for his written, short meditations	Most important art style of the 1600s	Term meaning strong contrasts between light and dark
Italian Baroque master of *chiaroscuro* (*Calling of St. Matthew*)	Most important female Baroque painter in Rome	Greatest Italian Baroque artist (*David; Ecstasy of St. Teresa*)

STUDY CARDS - Place your answers in the spaces below. ✂

_ _ _ _ _	_ _ _ _ _ _ _ _ _	_ _ _ _ _ _ _ _ _ _ _
_ _ _ _	_ _ _ _ _ _ _ _ _ _ _ _ _ _ _	_ _ _ _ _ _
_ _ _ _ _ _	_ _ _ _ _ _ _ _ _	_ _ _ _ _ _ _ _ _
_ _ _ _ _ _	_ _ _ _ _ _ _	_ _ _ _ _ _
_ _ _ _ _ _ _ _ _ _ _	_ _ _ _ _ _ _	_ _ _ _ _ _ _
_ _ _ _ _ _	_ _ _ _ _	_ _ _ _ _

STUDY CARDS - 19th & 20th CENTURIES - B

French Impressionist painter of ballet and theater (*The Rehearsal*)	French pointillist (*Sunday Afternoon on La Grande Jatte*)	Post-impressionist painter of Tahitians (*Ia Orana Maria*)
Dutch Post-impressionist (*Starry Night; The Night Cafe*)	Post-impressionist seeking geometric order (*Mont Saint-Victoire*)	Greatest sculptor of the 1800s (*The Kiss; Balzac*)
Russian novelist of realism and psychology (*Crime and Punishment*)	Norwegian Realist playwright (*A Doll's House*)	Norwegian Expressionist artist (*The Scream*)
Russian pioneer of non-representational art (*Several Circles*)	Term applied to French artists (like Matisse) who pauinted like "wild beasts"	Two founders of Cubism
Picasso's greatest painting of social protest	Protest art of Marcel Duchamp	Russian-born artist of dream-like images from his youth (*Green Violinist*)
French "stream-of consciousness" writer (*Remembrance of Things Past*)	Disillusioning event from 1914 to 1918	Author of "things fall apart, the centre cannot hold" ("The Second Coming")

STUDY CARDS - Place your answers in the spaces below. ✂

_ _ _ _ _ _ _	_ _ _ _ _ _	_ _ _ _ _
_ _ _ _ _	_ _ _ _ _ _ _	_ _ _ _ _ _ _
_ _ _ _ _	_ _ _ _ _	_ _ _ _ _ _ _ _ _ _
_ _ _ _ _ _ _ & _ _ _ _ _ _	_ _ _ _ _ _ _	_ _ _ _ _ _ _ _ _
_ _ _ _ _ _ _	_ _ _ _ _ _ _	_ _ _ _ _ _ _ _
_ _ _ _ _	_ _ _ _ _ _ _ _ _ _ _	_ _ _ _ _ _

STUDY CARDS - 19th & 20th CENTURIES - C

Czech "kafkaesque" author (*The Trial*)	Inventor of montage in movies (*Potemkin*)	Most important Spanish Surrealist (*Persistence of Memory*)
Belgian Surrealist (*Man with a Newspaper;* *This is Not A Pipe*)	Philosophy associated with Jean-Paul Sartre	Austrian psychotherapist: humans are irrational
American painter of urban loneliness (*Nighthawks*)	American painter of flowers and desert scenes (*Poppy*)	Capital city of art in the 1920s
Capital city of art in the 1950s	American Abstract Expressionist (*Number 1, 1948*)	American Pop Artist (*Mick Jagger*)
Artist of "mobiles" (*Big Red*)	American architect: (Guggenheim Museum)	Modern architect from Germany's Bauhaus School (Seagram Building, New York)
Playwright of the "Theater of the Absurd" (*Waiting for Godot*)	Swedish film director (*Wild Strawberries,* *The Seventh Seal)*	Architect of the National Gallery East Building and of the Louvre Pyramid

STUDY CARDS - Place your answers in the spaces below. ✂

_ _ _ _	_ _ _ _ _ _ _ _ _ _ _ _	_ _ _ _ _
_ _ _ _ _	_ _ _ _ _ _ _ _ _ _ _ _ _ _ _ _	_ _ _ _ _ _ _ _ _
_ _ _ _ _	_ ' _ _ _ _ _ _ _ _	_ _ _ _ _ _
_ _ _ _ _ _	_ _ _ _ _ _ _ _	_ _ _ _ _ _ _
_ _ _ _ _ _ _ _ _ _ _ _ _ _	_ _ _ _ _ _	_ _ _ _ _ _
_ _ _	_ _ _ _ _ _ _ _	_ _ _ _ _ _ _ _

STUDY CARDS - 19th & 20th CENTURIES - D

Indian spiritual and nationalist leader using "nonviolence"	"Imperial City" and "Forbidden City" of China	Subject of Britain's 1839-1842 war with China
Traditional capital of Japan	Religion native to Japan	Japanese novel (c.1015) written by Lady Murasaki
Name for Japanese professional warrior	Japanese Buddhism; known for sudden insights	Japanese poetry in 3 lines and 17 syllables
First important kingdom in West Africa	Great stone ruins in southern Africa	Literary movement and cultural consciousness of Leopold Senghor
First Africa novelist; *Chaka*, 1912	Most-widely read African novelist; *Things Fall Apart*, 1948	African winner of the Nobel Prize for Literature, 1986
Japanese director of *Rashomon*, 1950	Indian director of *The Apu Trilogy*, 1955-1958	Chinese director of *Story of Qui Ju*, 1992

STUDY CARDS - Place your answers in the spaces below. ✂

_ _ _ _ _	_ _ _ _ _ _ _	_ _ _ _ _ _
_ _ _ _ _ _ _ _ _ _ _	_ _ _ _ _ _	_ _ _ _ _
_ _ _ _ _	_ _ _	_ _ _ _ _ _ _
_ _ _ _ _ _ _ _ _	_ _ _ _ _ _ _ _	_ _ _ _ _
_ _ _ _ _ _ _	_ _ _ _ _ _	_ _ _ _ _ _
_ _ _ _ _	_ _ _	_ _ _ _ _ _ _ _